FORGIVING A CO-PARENT

21-Day Journal for Rebuilding Trust, Cultivating Cooperation, and Creating a Harmonious Family Dynamic

Blending Our Love, Maryland

Copyright © 2023 by Tuniscia Okeke

Cover Design

Published 2023

Library of Congress Cataloging-in-Publication Data has been applied for.

ISBN 978-1-962748-00-1 (Print)

ISBN 978-1-962748-01-8 (eBook)

Printed in the United States of America

FORGIVING A CO-PARENT

*21-Day Journal for Rebuilding Trust,
Cultivating Cooperation, and Creating
a Harmonious Family Dynamic*

TUNISCIA OKEKE

BLENDING OUR LOVE, INC.

DEDICATION

For our children's sake, we forgive and mend,

In unity, their hearts we'll tend.

Co-parenting with love's embrace,

Their future's grace we'll chase.

Table of Contents

Paying It Forward

I'm sharing this message as the author of this 21-day journal on forgiveness, not just with words on these pages but with a story that has shaped my life's purpose. As I embark on this journey with you, I want to share the deeply personal and transformative experiences that led me to write, edit, and self-publish 35 journals on forgiveness in less than a year.

My forgiveness journey began when I was 24, a pivotal age when life often feels like an open book, brimming with hope and dreams. Then, my mother called me on a seemingly ordinary Monday morning, and with those words, she unraveled the narrative of my life. She revealed that the man I had believed to be my father for all those years was, in fact, not my biological father.

The weight of that revelation was crushing. It was as if the ground beneath me had shifted, leaving me unsteady and disoriented. But what shook me to my core was not the revelation itself but the sudden rupture of trust in my mother—the person I had always looked up to as a paragon of love, trustworthiness, and honesty.

In the wake of this revelation, I spiraled into a deep pit of resentment, anger, and pain. I grappled with a profound sense of betrayal and felt adrift in a sea of unanswered questions. It was a turbulent period in my life, and for 17 long years, I carried the heavy burden of unforgiveness.

Then, something remarkable happened that would alter the course of my life forever. I noticed a pattern in my relationship with my children. They treated me with a lack of respect and love, leaving me bewildered and hurt. In desperation, I turned to prayer one day, seeking answers from a higher source.

God's voice whispered into my heart in that sacred space of prayer and introspection, revealing a profound truth: "I taught them how to love me by the way I loved my mother."

Those words struck me like lightning, piercing through the fog of my confusion. It was an awakening—a profound realization that, in my quest for revenge against my mother, I had unwittingly passed on the energy of resentment to my children. I had normalized my hurtful behaviors as the way we should treat our mothers.

On my 40th birthday, I consciously confronted my soul's deepest and darkest corners. I embarked on a journey of healing, self-forgiveness, and forgiveness of my mother. My primary motivation was to restore my relationship with my children and teach them how to pass on healing, love, and forgiveness to their children.

That six-year odyssey of healing was transformative beyond measure. It led me to write 35 journals, each addressing a facet of forgiveness and healing I encountered on my journey. These journals became my way of reaching out to others grappling with their forgiveness journeys.

Today, I extend a heartfelt invitation to you to embark on this 21-day journey with me. Just as my healing journey began with a single journal, this journal can be your compass for forgiveness, healing, and growth.

I send you loving energy as you navigate through the complexities of your forgiveness journey, and I hope these pages serve as a guiding light toward wholeness and inner peace.

With love and compassion,

Tuniscia O

FOREWORD

A Heartfelt Letter from the Author

Dear Cherished Readers,

I extend my warmest greetings and heartfelt appreciation as we embark on a transformative journey through the pages of our 21-day journal, "Forgiving a Co-parent: Rebuilding Trust, Cultivating Cooperation, and Creating a Harmonious Co-parenting Family Dynamic."

Navigating the intricacies of co-parenting can be one of life's most challenging endeavors. Yet, it is also a profound opportunity for growth, healing, and the forging of a harmonious family dynamic.

This journal represents more than an author's words; it's a shared commitment to understanding, forgiveness, and unwavering love for our children. It is a testament to the transformative power of forgiveness in co-parenting.

Through these pages, we will embark on a healing journey, acknowledging that forgiveness is the cornerstone upon which trust is rebuilt. Through cooperation and understanding, we create a nurturing environment for our children, one in which they can thrive despite the complexities of our relationships.

You are not alone on this path. Within these pages, you will find stories of resilience, exercises to foster cooperation, and a supportive community of kindred spirits, all dedicated to the art of forgiveness and the well-being of our children.

With heartfelt gratitude for your commitment to healing, cooperation, and creating a harmonious co-parenting family,

Warmly,

Tuniscia O

Reclaiming Harmony

Introduction

C o-parenting, you embark on a profound journey—a journey towards forgiveness, the establishment of healthy boundaries, and healing. It's a path that can create a harmonious family dynamic despite the inevitable complexities.

It's a delicate dance, a symphony of shared responsibilities and emotions. You and your co-parent bring your unique perspectives and histories to the table. It's a journey marked by challenges, but within those challenges lies a profound opportunity for growth and unity.

Forgiveness is your compass on this journey. As you navigate the sometimes turbulent waters of co-parenting, forgiving your co-parent and yourself can be transformative. It's not about erasing the past but releasing its hold on your present and future.

Establishing healthy boundaries is your armor. It's about protecting your emotional and mental well-being while fostering cooperation and respect. Boundaries create the space where healing can occur, ensuring you maintain your sense of self within the co-parenting relationship.

Healing is your destination. It's where you release the weight of past grievances and step into a brighter future for your children. Healing enables growth and unity, transforming the sometimes turbulent co-parenting journey into a harmonious family dynamic.

As you embark on this transformative path, remember that forgiveness, boundaries, and healing are not destinations but ongoing processes. Each step brings you closer to the harmonious family dynamic you aspire to create—a dynamic filled with understanding, empathy, and a shared commitment to your children's well-being.

Navigating Co-Parenting with Grace and Healing

In co-parenting, forgiveness is a beacon of hope that illuminates the path toward grace and healing. It's a powerful choice that transcends anger and resentment, allowing you to regain control over your emotional well-being.

Forgiveness is not a pardon for past wrongs but a liberation from the emotional chains that bind you. Through forgiveness, you break free from the weight of grudges and anger, creating space for compassion and understanding to thrive. It's a journey that takes you from a place of hurt to one of healing, from discord to harmony.

As you explore the profound impact of forgiveness in the context of co-parenting, you'll discover how it opens doors to healthier communication, improved cooperation, and a more stable environment for your children. It's a courageous step toward rebuilding fractured relationships and nurturing a co-parenting dynamic marked by grace and healing.

Through the insights, you'll gain a deeper understanding of forgiveness as a tool for personal growth and transformation. It's not only a gift you extend to your co-parent but also a gift to yourself, a pathway to emotional liberation and the possibility of a more peaceful and harmonious co-parenting journey.

Acknowledging Hurt

Acknowledging hurt is the essential first step in healing and co-parenting with grace. It's a courageous act of self-awareness that allows you to confront the pain and turmoil caused by your co-parent's actions. By admitting your feelings without judgment, you create a safe space within yourself to process and understand the emotional weight burdening you.

This acknowledgment is not a sign of weakness but a testament to your strength and resilience. It's an honest confrontation with your emotions, a recognition that you have been affected deeply by the challenges of co-parenting. Through this process, you honor your experiences and give yourself permission to heal.

Acknowledging hurt paves the way for open and honest communication with your co-parent. It's the foundation for building a more collaborative and understanding co-parenting dynamic. It's also vital in releasing resentment and making room for forgiveness.

Remember that acknowledging hurt is not a one-time event; it's an ongoing practice of self-compassion and self-discovery. As you navigate the complexities of co-parenting, allow yourself the space and time to acknowledge your feelings, process your emotions, and ultimately find the healing and grace you seek in this journey.

Self-Compassion

Self-compassion is a crucial aspect of the forgiveness journey, especially in the context of co-parenting challenges. It's about extending the same understanding and kindness to yourself that you would offer to a dear friend facing a similar situation.

In the complex and often emotionally charged world of co-parenting, it's natural to experience a wide range of emotions – anger, frustration, sadness, and even moments of self-doubt. Self-compassion invites you to acknowledge these emotions without judgment. It allows you to understand that forgiveness is a deeply personal and sometimes turbulent journey, and feeling these emotions is okay.

Imagine a close friend going through a similar co-parenting struggle. You can offer them words of comfort, encouragement, and support. Self-compassion urges you to do the same for yourself. Instead of being critical or overly demanding, it encourages you to be gentle and patient with your emotional responses.

By practicing self-compassion, you create a nurturing environment within yourself, one that fosters healing and personal growth. It helps you navigate the complexities of co-parenting with greater resilience and self-acceptance, ultimately paving the way for a more harmonious and forgiving co-parenting relationship. Remember, the journey to forgiveness begins within, and self-compassion is your steadfast companion.

Release Resentment

Releasing resentment is a vital step in the journey of forgiveness, especially in the context of co-parenting challenges. Resentment is like a heavy anchor, weighing down your emotional well-being and hindering progress toward a healthier co-parenting relationship.

It's crucial to recognize that letting go of resentment doesn't mean condoning or justifying the actions that led to it. Instead, it's a choice to liberate yourself from these feelings' emotional grip on you. When you hold onto resentment, it's like carrying a burden that grows heavier with time, sapping your energy and hindering your ability to move forward.

By releasing resentment, you are not excusing the behaviors or actions of your co-parent. You are choosing to break free from the cycle of pain and emotional turmoil that resentment perpetuates. Letting go is a decisive step towards reclaiming your emotional well-being and finding the space to work towards a more cooperative and harmonious co-parenting dynamic.

Forgiveness doesn't erase the past but allows you to create a future that isn't overshadowed by bitterness and anger. It's a gift you give to yourself, one that opens the door to healing and the possibility of a more peaceful co-parenting relationship, ultimately benefiting both you and your children.

Cultivating Empathy

Cultivating empathy in co-parenting can be a transformative and healing process. It's about extending yourself to understand your co-parent's perspective, even if you strongly disagree with their actions or decisions. Empathy doesn't mean condoning their behavior, but it does humanize their motivations and struggles.

When you foster empathy, you create a bridge of understanding between yourself and your co-parent. This doesn't imply that you have to agree with or accept their actions, but it allows you to see them as a complex individual with their challenges and experiences.

By attempting to understand their perspective, you open the door to more constructive communication and a potential path toward forgiveness. It's a step towards depersonalizing the conflicts and recognizing that people are often driven by various factors, including their fears, insecurities, and past traumas.

Empathy is a powerful tool in co-parenting because it can lead to more compassionate and productive interactions. It enables you to approach disagreements with a mindset of curiosity and a genuine desire to find common ground or solutions that prioritize the well-being of your children.

Ultimately, fostering empathy is an act of self-empowerment as well. It allows you to rise above the anger and resentment often accompanying co-parenting challenges and choose a path of healing and understanding for your co-parent and yourself.

The Art of Communication

The art of effective communication stands as a cornerstone in the realm of co-parenting, serving as the bridge that connects forgiveness with healing. Its significance lies in its pivotal role in navigating the intricate landscape of co-parenting challenges.

Remember that effective communication transcends the mere exchange of words. It delves deeper, encompassing the profound acts of genuine listening, heartfelt empathy, and the skillful expression of thoughts and emotions. Through this art, you foster not just conversation but understanding and collaboration.

In the world of co-parenting, open and honest dialogue becomes your compass, guiding you through the complexities of shared responsibilities and emotions. It provides a channel for your children to witness respect, cooperation, and the power of resolution. It is through effective communication that you create a safe space where both you and your co-parent can express your feelings, concerns, and aspirations.

Mastering this art strengthens your co-parenting partnership and paves the way for healing and growth. You lay the foundation for forgiveness by acknowledging each other's perspectives and working together to build a harmonious co-parenting environment. In doing so, you benefit yourselves and create a nurturing atmosphere where your children can thrive, free from the burdens of conflict and division.

Active Listening

Active listening is a foundational skill in the realm of co-parenting. It's a practice that goes beyond hearing words; it involves fully engaging with what your co-parent is saying, understanding their perspective, and validating their feelings. Active listening can significantly contribute to effective communication and conflict resolution in co-parenting.

When you actively listen to your co-parent, you create a safe and respectful space for them to express their thoughts and emotions. This, in turn, encourages open dialogue and fosters a sense of understanding and empathy between both parties. It's about being present in the moment, putting aside your agenda or defensiveness, and genuinely seeking to comprehend their point of view.

Furthermore, active listening involves validating your co-parent's feelings and experiences. Even if you don't necessarily agree with their perspective, acknowledging their emotions as valid can go a long way in building trust and goodwill in your co-parenting relationship.

Encouraging your co-parent to share openly without interruption is another key aspect of active listening. Allowing them to express themselves fully without fear of judgment can lead to more productive and meaningful conversations.

Incorporating active listening into your co-parenting interactions can help reduce misunderstandings, defuse conflicts, and create a more harmonious co-parenting dynamic. It's a powerful tool for nurturing empathy, understanding, and effective communication in raising children.

Expressing Your Feelings

Expressing your feelings is a crucial component of effective co-parenting communication. It's about sharing your emotions, needs, and concerns clearly and respectfully, creating an environment where you and your co-parent can engage in constructive dialogue.

One helpful approach is to use "I" statements when communicating your feelings. Instead of saying, "You never listen to me," which can come across as accusatory, you might say, "I feel unheard and frustrated when I don't think my perspective is considered." "I" statements focus on your emotions and experiences, allowing you to express yourself without assigning blame.

This technique makes you more likely to foster a safe, open, honest conversation space. It reduces defensiveness and encourages your co-parent to listen and understand your point of view. Additionally, it helps prevent conversations from escalating into conflicts, as "I" statements emphasize your feelings rather than making sweeping judgments about your co-parent's behavior.

Effective co-parenting relies on clear and respectful communication. Expressing your feelings with care and using "I" statements can help you navigate challenges and conflicts while maintaining a healthy co-parenting relationship focused on the well-being of your children. It's a valuable tool for fostering understanding and cooperation in the shared journey of raising your kids.

Setting Boundaries

Setting boundaries is a fundamental aspect of successful co-parenting. It involves establishing clear guidelines for communication and interactions, with a primary focus on the well-being of your children. These boundaries serve several essential purposes in the co-parenting dynamic.

First and foremost, boundaries protect your emotional well-being. They create a buffer between you and your co-parent, ensuring conversations and interactions don't veer into emotionally charged or harmful territory. You safeguard your mental and emotional space by defining what is acceptable and what isn't in your co-parenting relationship.

Secondly, boundaries encourage constructive interaction. When both parties understand the rules and limitations of communication, it becomes easier to engage in discussions related to your children's needs without getting sidetracked by personal conflicts or disagreements. This fosters a more productive and harmonious co-parenting environment.

Additionally, boundaries help maintain a sense of respect and civility in your interactions with your co-parent. By clearly defining what is expected and acceptable behavior, you set the tone for a relationship built on mutual respect, even if personal feelings may differ.

Setting boundaries is a proactive step in ensuring that your co-parenting journey focuses on providing your children with the best possible upbringing. It allows both parties to navigate the challenges of co-parenting with clarity, respect, and emotional well-being intact.

Shared Responsibility

Shared responsibility is at the heart of successful co-parenting. It involves a collaborative and cooperative approach where parents actively make decisions and care for their children's well-being. This approach is built on several fundamental principles contributing to a harmonious co-parenting relationship.

It is recognizing the equal importance of both parents in the children's lives. It acknowledges that each parent brings unique strengths, perspectives, and experiences to the co-parenting dynamic. This recognition fosters an atmosphere of mutual respect and cooperation.

Having a responsibility encourages open communication and decision-making. It means involving parents in discussions about important aspects of their children's lives, such as education, healthcare, and extracurricular activities. Including both perspectives ensures that the children's best interests are at the forefront of decision-making.

Additionally, shared responsibility promotes consistency and stability for the children. Both parents are actively engaged and share parenting responsibilities, providing security and continuity.

In essence, shared responsibility in co-parenting is about working together as a team to provide the best possible upbringing for your children. It requires effective communication, mutual respect, and a commitment to meeting children's needs. When both parents actively share parenting responsibilities, it creates a positive and nurturing environment for the children to thrive.

Identifying Needs

Identifying needs is fundamental in establishing healthy boundaries within a co-parenting relationship. Recognizing your emotional requirements, values, and priorities requires introspection and self-awareness.

Understanding your emotional needs is crucial. Consider what brings you a sense of emotional well-being and what triggers stress or discomfort. For example, you may need regular communication about your child's welfare to feel secure or require space and autonomy to maintain your emotional balance. Identifying these needs allows you to set boundaries that protect and prioritize your emotional health.

Your values play a significant role in boundary-setting. What principles and beliefs guide your decisions as a co-parent? Whether it's a commitment to open and respectful communication or a dedication to fostering a positive environment for your child, aligning your boundaries with your values ensures that your co-parenting dynamic is consistent with your core beliefs.

Prioritizing your needs helps you strike a balance between co-parenting responsibilities and self-care. It allows you to communicate your requirements clearly and respectfully to your co-parent, fostering an environment where both parties can meet their needs without compromising the child's well-being.

By identifying your emotional needs, values, and priorities, you empower yourself to establish boundaries that promote emotional well-being and contribute to a harmonious co-parenting relationship. These boundaries protect your mental and emotional health and create a stable and nurturing environment for your child's growth and development.

Boundaries Are Your Friend

Welcoming boundaries is a crucial aspect of co-parenting that contributes to a healthier and more harmonious relationship between separated or divorced parents. Boundaries serve as the framework for defining roles, responsibilities, and acceptable behaviors within the co-parenting dynamic.

Establishing boundaries helps create a sense of structure and predictability for parents and children. When each parent knows their respective roles and responsibilities, it reduces confusion and potential conflicts. For example, clearly defining who is responsible for school-related matters, healthcare decisions, or visitation schedules can help prevent misunderstandings and disputes.

Furthermore, boundaries protect emotional well-being. They enable parents to set limits on intrusive or disrespectful behaviors, fostering an environment of respect and consideration. For instance, boundaries can include guidelines for communication, ensuring that interactions remain civil and focused on the children's best interests.

Embracing boundaries also encourages personal growth and self-care. By recognizing your limits and needs, you can take steps to prioritize your emotional and mental health. This, in turn, benefits your children by providing them with a more emotionally stable and resilient parent.

In essence, boundaries are the cornerstone of effective co-parenting. They provide a clear roadmap for navigating the challenges of raising children separately while maintaining a respectful and cooperative relationship. By embracing boundaries, both parents can create a positive and nurturing co-parenting environment that benefits the well-being and development of their children.

Communicate Boundaries

Effective co-parenting relies on clear and respectful communication of boundaries. It's essential to convey your boundaries to your co-parent in a way that fosters understanding and cooperation. Here are some key steps to effectively communicate your boundaries:

Choose the Right Time and Place

Find an appropriate and private setting to discuss your boundaries. Avoid addressing these matters during high-conflict situations or in front of your child.

Be Direct and Specific

Clearly state your boundaries without ambiguity. Use "I" statements to express your needs and expectations. For example, say, "I need us to communicate about our child's schedule through text messages only," instead of "You should stop calling me."

Explain the Why

Help your co-parent understand the reasons behind your boundaries. Sharing your motivations can create empathy and cooperation. For instance, "I prefer written communication to avoid misunderstandings and conflicts."

Listen Actively

Allow your co-parent to express their thoughts and concerns as well. Active listening fosters a respectful dialogue and can lead to compromises that work for both parties.

Emphasize Cooperation

Stress that these boundaries are meant to create a more harmonious co-parenting relationship and prioritize the child's well-being. Make it clear that you are open to discussing and adjusting the boundaries as needed.

Document Agreements

After discussing boundaries, it can be helpful to document them in a co-parenting agreement or plan that both parties agree to follow. This formalizes the boundaries and serves as a reference point in disputes.

Be Consistent

Once boundaries are established, consistently adhere to them. Consistency builds trust and reinforces the importance of respecting each other's limits.

Effective communication of boundaries is essential for creating a respectful, cooperative, co-parenting environment that focuses on the child's best interests. It helps both parties understand their needs and expectations, creating a more harmonious and functional co-parenting relationship.

Enforce Boundaries

Enforcing boundaries when crossed in a co-parenting situation is crucial for maintaining a healthy and respectful dynamic. Here are steps to effectively handle boundary violations:

Immediate Communication: Address the violation promptly. Contact your co-parent to express your concerns calmly and assertively. Use "I" statements to describe your feelings and the impact of the boundary breach.

Set Clear Consequences: Communicate the consequences for crossing boundaries in your co-parenting agreement or guidelines. Ensure both parties understand the repercussions, such as altering visitation schedules or involving a mediator.

Document Violations: Keep records of boundary violations, including dates, times, and details of the incidents. This documentation can be valuable if you must involve legal authorities or mediators.

Consult a Mediator or Therapist: If communication breaks down or boundary violations persist, consider involving a neutral third party, such as a mediator or therapist, to facilitate discussions and resolutions.

Maintain Consistency: Enforce boundaries consistently to establish trust and predictability in the co-parenting relationship. Consistency helps both parties understand the importance of respecting each other's limits.

Self-Care: Focus on self-care to manage the emotional toll of boundary violations. Seek support from friends, family, or a therapist to help you navigate the challenges.

Reevaluate and Adjust: Periodically review and adjust your co-parenting boundaries as needed. Life circumstances change, and adjustments may be necessary to accommodate new situations.

Focus on the Child: Always keep the child's well-being at the forefront of your efforts. Remind yourself and your co-parent that boundaries are established to create a stable and nurturing environment for your child.

Enforcing boundaries when they are crossed requires patience, effective communication, and a commitment to resolving conflicts while prioritizing the child's best interests. It's a challenging but essential aspect of co-parenting that contributes to a more harmonious and supportive co-parenting relationship.

Consistency With Boundaries

Consistency is the cornerstone of effective boundary maintenance in co-parenting. It involves a delicate balance between firmness and flexibility. While standing by the boundaries you've established is essential, it's equally important to recognize when adjustments are necessary. This balance ensures that the emotional well-being of both co-parents and the children's best interests remain at the forefront.

Being consistent in upholding boundaries provides a sense of predictability and security within the co-parenting dynamic. It fosters trust between both parties and minimizes the potential for conflicts to arise. Children, in particular, benefit from this stability, as it contributes to their emotional security during the often challenging transitions of co-parenting.

However, it's essential to acknowledge that life is dynamic, and circumstances may change. Remaining open to necessary adjustments demonstrates a willingness to adapt to evolving needs. Flexibility within the framework of established boundaries ensures that co-parenting remains effective and responsive to the ever-changing needs of the children and co-parents themselves.

In summary, consistency in maintaining boundaries is about finding the equilibrium between steadfastness and adaptability. It's a commitment to the well-being of all involved parties, allowing co-parents to navigate the complex journey of co-parenting with resilience and empathy.

Nurturing Healing and Growth

In the intricate dance of co-parenting, forgiveness and boundaries are your guiding stars, illuminating the path toward healing and growth. They form the foundation for building a resilient and thriving co-parenting dynamic.

Forgiveness is the key that unlocks the door to healing. By forgiving your co-parent and yourself, you release the burdens of the past, making space for transformation. It's a process that requires courage and compassion, allowing you to let go of old wounds and embrace the potential for a brighter future.

Boundaries are your protective shield on this journey. They safeguard your emotional well-being, ensuring you have the space and stability needed for growth. Healthy boundaries establish the ground rules for respectful and cooperative co-parenting, creating an environment where you and your children can flourish.

As you nurture healing and growth, resilience becomes your trusted companion. The strength carries you through challenges and setbacks, reminding you of your capacity to overcome adversity. Self-care becomes a sacred ritual, replenishing your spirit and enabling you to show up as the best version of yourself for your children.

Embracing personal change is your secret weapon for positive transformation. It's the willingness to adapt, learn, and grow as a co-parent. A positive mindset becomes your daily armor, shaping your perspective and guiding your actions toward fostering an environment where you and your children survive and thrive.

In this co-parenting journey, healing and growth are not mere aspirations but your birthright. With forgiveness as your compass and boundaries as your anchor, you can create a nurturing space where you and your children can flourish, resilient in the face of life's challenges and ever-reaching for the bright horizon of the future.

Self-Care

Self-care is not a luxury but a vital component of your well-being, especially when navigating the intricate terrain of co-parenting. It's easy to prioritize your children's needs and the demands of co-parenting over your own, but neglecting self-care can lead to emotional burnout and strained relationships.

Establishing and maintaining boundaries in co-parenting can be emotionally taxing. That's why it's crucial to prioritize self-care. Self-care isn't selfish; it's a means of recharging and preserving your mental and emotional health.

Allocate time in your schedule for activities that bring you joy and relaxation. Whether it's practicing mindfulness, engaging in hobbies, or spending quality time with loved ones, these moments of rejuvenation are essential for your overall well-being.

Prioritizing self-care not only benefits you but also positively impacts your co-parenting relationship. When you approach co-parenting with a centered and positive mindset, you're better equipped to communicate effectively and make decisions in the best interests of your children.

Remember that self-care is an ongoing practice. It's not something you do sporadically but a consistent commitment to nurturing your emotional and mental health. Caring for yourself sets a positive example for your children and creates a healthier co-parenting dynamic for everyone involved.

Embracing Change

Embracing change is a fundamental aspect of personal growth and your co-parenting relationship's evolution. Change can be daunting, especially when it involves navigating the complexities of co-parenting after separation or divorce. However, it's essential to recognize that change is a natural and necessary part of life.

As you embark on this co-parenting journey, understand that healing and growth often require change. You may need to adapt your communication styles, adjust your expectations, or shift your perspective to foster a more positive co-parenting dynamic. Embracing these changes can lead to more effective and harmonious interactions with your co-parent.

Personal growth is an ongoing process, and change is at its core. Embracing change means being open to new experiences, learning from past mistakes, and continually evolving. This growth benefits you and positively influences your co-parenting relationship and, most importantly, your children.

While change can be challenging, it's a catalyst for positive transformation. Embrace it as an opportunity for healing, personal development, and creating a healthier co-parenting environment. Remember that change is not a sign of weakness but a testament to your resilience and willingness to work toward a brighter future for yourself and your children.

Positive Mindset

Cultivating a positive mindset is a powerful tool in co-parenting. It involves shifting your perspective to focus on the lessons learned from challenges rather than dwelling on the difficulties themselves. When you approach co-parenting with optimism, you acknowledge that each day presents an opportunity for growth and positive change.

A positive mindset allows you to see setbacks as stepping stones toward improvement rather than insurmountable obstacles. It enables you to view co-parenting not as a burden but as a chance to model resilience and emotional maturity for your children.

By embracing a positive mindset, you open yourself up to finding common ground with your co-parent, even in the face of differences. It encourages effective communication, as you are more likely to seek solutions and compromise when approaching challenges with a constructive attitude.

Remember that a positive mindset is a choice you make daily. It's about recognizing that co-parenting may have complexities, but your approach can be infused with hope, understanding, and a commitment to personal and familial growth. Doing so creates a healthier co-parenting environment that benefits you and your children.

Modeling Emotional Health

Modeling emotional health in the context of co-parenting is a valuable lesson for your children. It involves demonstrating emotional intelligence by effectively processing and healthily communicating your feelings. Doing so enhances your well-being and provides your children with a positive example of navigating complex emotions.

Children learn by observing, and when they see their co-parents handling emotions with maturity and respect, they are more likely to adopt similar behaviors. This includes recognizing and expressing feelings without blame or judgment, which fosters open and honest communication.

Also, modeling emotional health extends to your co-parenting relationship. When you prioritize a balanced and cooperative dynamic, you show your children that conflicts can be resolved through understanding and compromise rather than hostility or animosity. This sets the stage for them to develop their healthy relationship skills in the future.

Healing-Centered Co-Parenting

Co-parenting is an intricate dance of shared responsibilities and mutual respect, but it can also stir up unresolved emotional wounds. It's vital to approach this journey from a space of healing rather than revenge, consciously making decisions that prioritize your child's well-being.

For many, co-parenting may trigger deep-seated pain from past experiences, particularly childhood rejection or abandonment. These emotions can easily resurface when faced with disagreements or challenges in co-parenting. However, it's crucial to recognize that using co-parenting as a battleground for revenge or retribution only perpetuates the cycle of hurt.

Healing-centered co-parenting involves self-awareness and mindfulness. It requires acknowledging the emotional triggers and actively working on addressing them. By being present in your healing process, you can break free from the shackles of past pain and create a more nurturing environment for your child.

Conscious decision-making is another cornerstone of healing-centered co-parenting. When faced with conflicts, pause and reflect before reacting. Ask yourself if your response is driven by past wounds or your child's well-being. Choosing the latter ensures your decisions are rooted in love and care rather than revenge.

Ultimately, healing-centered co-parenting is a powerful testament to your growth and resilience. It sets a positive example for your child, showing them the importance of healing, forgiveness, and prioritizing their needs. By consciously embracing this approach, you pave the way for a brighter future built on love, compassion, and a commitment to breaking the cycle of pain.

Journaling For Success

A 21-Day Forgiveness and Healing Journal provides a structured pathway to release the past, embrace empathy, and nurture forgiveness in co-parenting. Through consistent reflection and introspection, you'll find yourself on a path toward healing, growth, and a renewed sense of harmony in your co-parenting relationship.

Journaling is a private canvas for self-discovery, healing, and growth, where your thoughts find a voice, emotions find solace, and clarity finds its home.

Here are some tips to help you thrive:

Consistency

Commit to journaling daily for the full 21 days. Consistency ensures you stay engaged with your emotions and progress towards forgiveness and healing.

Honesty

Be honest and transparent with yourself. Use your journal as a safe space to confront your feelings, doubts, and fears.

Gratitude

Incorporate gratitude into your entries. Write down something you're grateful for each day, whether it's a small positive interaction with your co-parent or a personal insight you've gained.

Self-Compassion

Approach the journaling process with self-compassion. Be kind to yourself as you navigate through challenging emotions, and celebrate your progress along the way.

Reflection

At the end of the 21 days, review your entries. Notice the evolution of your thoughts, feelings, and perspectives. Use this reflection to guide your ongoing journey of forgiveness and healing.

So, pick up your pen and let it dance across the pages. Let the ink weave a tapestry of healing and empowerment—an intimate conversation with yourself that leads to renewal. Embrace the transformative power of journaling and step into a future where you stand tall, unburdened by the weight of wounds, and radiate with the radiance of self-love and the beauty of your unique journey.

I Forgive Myself For Making Excuses For Your Behavior

Forgiveness Reflection of the Day

Reflecting on my journey towards forgiving myself for making excuses for my co-parent's behavior, I am at a crossroads of emotions. This process has been challenging and liberating, allowing me to delve deep into my psyche and confront the patterns that have held me back. Forgiveness is difficult, especially when it involves acknowledging my complicity in enabling my co-parent's actions. However, I understand that by forgiving myself, I can break free from the cycle of excuses and pave the way for a healthier co-parenting relationship.

At the heart of my self-forgiveness journey lies the recognition that making excuses for my co-parent's behavior was born out of fear and a desperate desire to avoid confrontation. I convinced myself that excusing their actions was the only way to maintain harmony for the sake of our children. But in doing so, I compromised my boundaries and self-respect. I allowed the cycle of enabling to continue, allowing my co-parent to avoid responsibility for their actions.

Recognizing my role in this dynamic was difficult but crucial. I had to confront my fears, insecurities, and doubts about my abilities as a co-parent. I had to acknowledge that my fear of conflict and losing control ultimately led me to make excuses for their behavior. As I explored these feelings, I understood that forgiving myself was not about condoning their actions but releasing myself from guilt and self-blame.

As I forgave myself, I also had to learn to set healthy boundaries with my co-parent. I realized that enabling their behavior harmed me and hindered their growth and development. By refusing to make excuses and holding them accountable, I encouraged them to take responsibility for their actions and seek help. In doing so, I fostered an environment where we could learn and grow as co-parents.

In this process, I also had to embrace self-compassion. Forgiving myself meant accepting that I am human, prone to mistakes, and learning from them. It meant allowing myself to feel the pain and disappointment caused by the excuses I made and understanding that these emotions were valid. However, I also learned that self-compassion does not equate to self-indulgence. It required taking responsibility for my actions and changing how I approached co-parenting.

As I forgive myself and let go of excuses, I also recognize the importance of communication and empathy in our co-parenting relationship. Open and honest dialogue is essential in understanding each other's perspectives and finding common ground. Empathy allows us to see beyond our emotions and comprehend the struggles that might lead to certain behaviors. While forgiveness does not justify or excuse their actions, it will enable me to separate the person from their behavior and focus on creating a more positive co-parenting environment.

This journey toward self-forgiveness has not been linear; there have been moments of doubt and relapses into old patterns. But I remind myself that this is all part of the process. Forgiveness is not a destination but an ongoing practice of self-awareness and growth.

Forgiving myself for making excuses for my co-parent's behavior has been a transformative journey. It required me to face my fears, set boundaries, embrace self-compassion, and engage in open communication and empathy. Through this process, I have learned that forgiveness does not mean condoning or forgetting the past; it means freeing myself from the weight of guilt and moving forward with a renewed commitment to healthy co-parenting. By embracing this journey, I am paving the way for a brighter and more fulfilling future for myself and my children.

Harmonious Meditative Thought of the Day

Today, I choose to let go of excuses for my co-parent's behavior. Instead, I embrace understanding and compassion. By releasing blame, I free myself to focus on creating a harmonious co-parenting environment for the well-being of our children.

Deeper Connection Within

I forgive my actions for being misleading to my children about _____

_____

_____.

I forgive myself and (co-parent) for manipulating me into lying to our children about _____

_____

_____.

I forgive myself for judging _____

_____

_____

_____.

Loving Statements About Me

I deserve healing and inner peace.

I release the weight of resentment and embrace a brighter future.

I forgive myself for any judgments or negative thoughts.

Gratitude Reflection of the Day

Today, I am grateful for the journey of co-parenting, which has allowed me to learn and understand myself more deeply, revealing the strength within me.

Inner Reflections

_____

_____

_____

_____

_____

_____

_____

_____

_____

_____

_____

_____

_____

_____

_____

_____

_____

I Forgive Myself For Ignoring The Red Flags While Co-Parenting

Forgiveness Reflection of the Day

Today, as I reflect on my journey towards forgiving myself for ignoring red flags in my co-parenting relationship, I am met with a mix of emotions – remorse and regret, a glimmer of hope. This process has been difficult, requiring me to confront my shortcomings and take responsibility for my choices. However, I understand that forgiveness is essential for my growth and the well-being of my children.

In hindsight, ignoring red flags in my co-parenting dynamic resulted from my deep desire for things to work smoothly and harmoniously. I yearned for a picture-perfect co-parenting arrangement where our children could thrive without witnessing conflict. Consequently, I downplay or overlook warning signs pointing to potential partnership issues.

Forgiving myself begins with acknowledging that I am not perfect and I am allowed to make mistakes. My decision to ignore the red flags stemmed from vulnerability and the fear of admitting that things might not be as idyllic as I wished. I must understand that self-forgiveness does not mean excusing my behavior but recognizing my humanity and committing to growth.

Recognizing the red flags I ignored is not easy, as it requires confronting uncomfortable truths about myself and my co-parenting dynamic. I must admit that I chose to turn a blind eye to inconsistencies in communication, lack of accountability, and emotional manipulation. In doing so, I allowed unhealthy patterns to persist, impacting my well-being and my children's.

Embracing forgiveness also involves understanding that co-parenting is a journey of continuous learning and adjustment. Ignoring red flags was an attempt to preserve the illusion of a perfect partnership, which hindered my ability to address underlying issues constructively. I must remind myself that acknowledging red flags is not a failure but an opportunity for growth and improvement.

One of the crucial steps towards self-forgiveness is learning from the mistakes I made. I failed to prioritize my children's and myself's well-being by ignoring red flags. As I move forward, I commit to becoming more vigilant and attentive to potential warning signs. I will strive to establish healthy boundaries, encourage open communication, and prioritize the safety and happiness of my children above all else.

Forgiving myself also means releasing the guilt and shame that have weighed heavily on my heart. While my decisions might have had negative consequences, I choose not to dwell on the past but instead focus on the present and the future. I can't change my mistakes, but can change how I respond to them now.

In this journey towards self-forgiveness, I am learning to practice self-compassion. It is crucial to be gentle with myself and to recognize that I, too, am a work in progress. I must resist the urge to criticize myself and replace negative self-talk with affirmations of growth and resilience. Embracing self-compassion allows me to see my mistakes as opportunities for learning and transformation.

As I forgive myself for ignoring red flags in co-parenting, I commit to being more attuned to my instincts and intuition. I will listen to my inner voice, even if it means confronting uncomfortable truths. By doing so, I will create a healthier and more balanced co-parenting relationship that fosters trust, understanding, and mutual respect.

Forgiving myself for ignoring red flags in co-parenting is an ongoing process of self-awareness, growth, and compassion. I am learning to accept my imperfections, acknowledge my mistakes, and take proactive steps to create a positive co-parenting environment for my children. By embracing forgiveness, I am giving myself the gift of healing and the opportunity to build a stronger foundation for the future.

Harmonious Meditative Thought of the Day

Reflecting on moments when I overlooked red flags in my co-parenting journey, I embrace the profound shift that accountability brings. Ignoring warning signs may have led to turbulence, but responsibility offers the compass to navigate these challenges differently. It's not about blame but understanding the lessons within each experience.

Accountability empowers me to acknowledge my role in past conflicts and to communicate openly and honestly. It invites a harmonious transformation, where we prioritize the well-being of our children and work collaboratively.

Through accountability, I choose to break the cycle of discord, replacing it with compassion, empathy, and a shared commitment to a harmonious co-parenting experience. Today, I step into this new chapter with the wisdom of reflection and the grace of accountability, fostering a co-parenting dynamic rooted in respect and cooperation.

Deeper Connection Within

I forgive myself for ignoring the red flags when _____

_____

_____

_____.

I forgive myself for not speaking up about _____

_____

_____

_____.

I forgive myself for not trusting my intuition when ____

_____

_____

_____.

Loving Statements About Me

My journey of forgiveness is a powerful act of self-love.

I am capable of healing and growing from this experience.

I choose to let go of the past and create a positive present.

Gratitude Reflection of the Day

I appreciate the moments of self-discovery that co-parenting has brought, helping me better understand my values, priorities, and the kind of parent I aspire to be.

Inner Reflections

Forgiving The Parental Alienation

Forgiveness Reflection of the Day

Today, as I embark on the journey of forgiving myself and my co-parent for the painful experience of parental alienation, I confront a rollercoaster of emotions. Parental alienation has torn at the very fabric of our family, leaving wounds that run deep. However, forgiveness is crucial to healing and rebuilding trust for our children's well-being.

In hindsight, my actions contributed to the development of parental alienation. As emotions ran high, I may have made decisions and uttered words that only fueled our divide. In pursuing self-preservation and the desire to prove my point, I inadvertently pushed my co-parent away from the children. Forgiving myself means understanding that I am human and imperfect, capable of making mistakes during emotional turmoil.

Reflecting on my co-parent's role in the alienation, I try to empathize with their struggles and emotions. Though their actions have caused pain and division, I understand they, too, might grapple with their fears, insecurities, and unresolved conflicts. Forgiveness does not excuse their behavior, but it allows me to find compassion and separate the person from the hurtful actions.

Forgiveness is not a single act but an ongoing daily commitment to release resentment and bitterness. As I choose to forgive myself and my co-parent, I understand that it does not mean forgetting the past but freeing myself from its grip. It means recognizing that the pain we experience can't be undone, but I can choose not to be defined by it.

One of the most challenging aspects of forgiveness is rebuilding trust. The breach caused by parental alienation has shattered the foundation of trust that our co-parenting relationship once stood on. However, with consistent effort and open communication, we can mend the trust and create a more stable environment for our children.

Forgiveness also involves learning from the past and committing to positive changes moving forward. I must acknowledge my actions' role in the alienation and consciously foster a healthier co-parenting dynamic. This means prioritizing the well-being of our children, setting aside personal grievances, and working towards shared parenting goals.

In the pursuit of forgiveness, I must embrace vulnerability. Opening up my heart to forgiveness means risking the possibility of being hurt again, but it also opens the door to healing and reconciliation. I choose to take this leap of faith because I believe in the transformative power of forgiveness, not only for myself but also for my co-parent and our children.

As I forgive, I focus on the present and the future rather than dwelling on past mistakes. I will embrace the opportunities to create new memories, nurture positive experiences, and foster an environment of love and acceptance for our children. I can start rebuilding the family bond strained by alienation by shifting my perspective.

Forgiveness is a gift I give not only to myself and my co-parent but also to our children. They deserve to grow up in an environment free from animosity and negativity. By forgiving and working towards reconciliation, I demonstrate to them the importance of empathy, compassion, and emotional resilience.

Forgiving myself and my co-parent for parental alienation is a profound and transformative process. It requires introspection, empathy, vulnerability, and a commitment to positive change. Through forgiveness, I hope to heal the wounds of the past, rebuild trust, and create a nurturing co-parenting environment that fosters the well-being and happiness of our children.

Harmonious Meditative Thought of the Day

Today, I embrace forgiving my co-parent for parental alienation. It's a journey into the depths of forgiveness, where I release the heavy burden of resentment and pain. Forgiving doesn't mean condoning the hurtful actions but liberating myself from their grip.

In forgiveness, I find the strength to break free from the cycle of alienation and foster a harmonious environment for our children. It's a conscious choice to prioritize their well-being above all else. Through forgiveness, I reclaim my power, transforming wounds into wisdom.

As I forgive, I open the door to healing and hope, creating space for cooperation and unity. It's a journey toward harmony, where love for our children precedes bitterness. Today, I choose forgiveness, knowing it is the path to a brighter, more harmonious co-parenting future.

Deeper Connection Within

I forgive myself for trying to get the children not to want to spend time with their other parent by telling them _____

_____

I forgive my mind for judging my co-parent for _____

_____

I forgive my mind for thinking my children should feel

_____

_____

towards their (mom/dad).

Loving Statements About Me

My heart is open to being understanding and empathic.

I am nurturing my emotional well-being with compassion.

Forgiveness liberates me from the burden of anger.

Gratitude Reflection of the Day

I'm thankful for the challenges and triumphs of co-parenting, as they have been opportunities for personal growth, resilience, and greater self-awareness.

I Forgive Myself For Not Enforcing Boundaries When They Are Ignored

Forgiveness Reflection of the Day

Today, as I engage in the daily practice of forgiveness, I focus on forgiving my co-parent for ignoring my boundaries. This process has been challenging and enlightening, forcing me to confront my frustration, disappointment, and hurt. However, I understand that forgiveness is essential to healing and nurturing a healthier co-parenting relationship.

Setting boundaries is crucial for maintaining a respectful and balanced co-parenting dynamic. It enables both parents to communicate openly, make decisions collaboratively, and prioritize the well-being of their children. But as I reflect on my co-parent's tendency to overlook my boundaries, I recognize that forgiveness is not about excusing their actions but finding peace within myself.

In the past, I hesitated to assert my boundaries clearly, fearing it might lead to conflict or jeopardize the stability of our co-parenting arrangement. I would bend and compromise, hoping to lead to a smoother coexistence. However, this lack of clear boundaries eroded my self-esteem and self-worth. I felt disregarded and disrespected, causing resentment to build.

Forgiving my co-parent begins with understanding that their actions might stem from their struggles and insecurities. It does not condone their behavior but allows me to detach my emotional well-being from their actions. I must recognize that I cannot control how they respond to my boundaries, but I can control how I react and protect my mental and emotional health.

As I engage in self-reflection, I also acknowledge my role in enabling the disregard of my boundaries. I realize that forgiveness involves letting go of self-blame and admitting that I can change the dynamic by being assertive and consistent in setting and enforcing my boundaries. By forgiving myself for not asserting my needs, I pave the way for growth and empowerment.

Forgiveness does not mean forgetting or repeating past mistakes. It means learning from the experience and using it as a catalyst for positive change. I commit to communicating my boundaries clearly and assertively, ensuring they are respected and honored. It may not always be easy, but it is essential for the health of our co-parenting relationship.

One of the most challenging aspects of forgiveness is finding empathy for my co-parent's perspective. Their failure to acknowledge my boundaries may result from their emotional struggles, past traumas, or misguided beliefs. As I strive to forgive, I attempt to view their actions through a lens of understanding, knowing that healing requires compassion.

Moving forward, I will work on setting healthy boundaries with kindness and firmness. I will seek professional support or mediation to facilitate productive conversations with my co-parent if necessary. Open communication can bridge the gap and help us find common ground in raising our children with love and respect.

Forgiveness also entails detaching from the past and living in the present. As I forgive my co-parent, I choose not to hold onto grudges or past grievances. Instead, I will build a positive co-parenting environment, prioritizing our children's emotional and psychological well-being.

Forgiving my co-parent for ignoring my boundaries is a transformative process that requires self-awareness, empathy, and commitment. I choose to forgive not for them but for myself and my children. I am fostering a co-parenting relationship grounded in mutual respect, communication, and love by setting and enforcing healthy boundaries. I take control of my emotional well-being through forgiveness and embrace the potential for a more positive and harmonious co-parenting journey.

Harmonious Meditative Thought of the Day

Today, I reflect on the harmonious art of enforcing boundaries when they are crossed. Boundaries are the loving fences we build around our well-being, and implementing them is an act of self-respect and self-care.

When we communicate and uphold our boundaries with clarity and compassion, we create an environment of mutual understanding and respect. It's not about building walls but rather fostering healthy connections.

Enforcing boundaries is a journey toward harmonious relationships. It allows us to protect our emotional and mental well-being while also respecting the autonomy and boundaries of others. It's a way to maintain balance and harmony in our interactions.

As I enforce my boundaries today, I do so with love and understanding, knowing that it's a vital step towards creating and maintaining harmonious connections in my life.

I forgive you for ignoring my boundaries.

Deeper Connection Within

I forgive myself for judging _____
_____ for ignoring my boundaries when
_____
_____ .

I forgive my mind for believing _____
_____ will never _____
_____
when co-parenting.

I forgive _____ for minimizing
my boundaries by _____
_____
_____ .

Loving Statements About Me

I am learning to forgive for my growth, not just for them.

I release the need to control the actions of others.

My strength comes from within, and I am resilient.

Gratitude Reflection of the Day

Today, I celebrate the moments of connection and cooperation with my co-parent, recognizing that every positive interaction brings us closer to the well-being of our children.

Inner Reflections

I Forgive You For The Lack Of Involvement

Forgiveness Reflection of the Day

Today's daily reflection centers on forgiving my co-parents for their lack of involvement in raising our children. This journey has been a bumpy road filled with emotions of frustration, disappointment, and sadness. However, I have realized that forgiveness is a powerful tool that can liberate me from the burden of resentment and pave the way for healing and growth.

When we became co-parents, I had hoped for a collaborative and equal partnership in raising our children. I imagined us working together, sharing responsibilities, and providing a stable and loving environment for them to thrive. However, over time, it became apparent that my co-parent needed to be more invested in the day-to-day upbringing of our children than I had hoped.

Forgiving my co-parent does not mean condoning their lack of involvement or excusing their actions. Instead, it means releasing their behavior's hold on my emotions and freeing myself from resentment. I acknowledge that they may have their reasons for not being as engaged as I would like them to be, but that doesn't invalidate my feelings or the impact of their choices on our children.

Self-forgiveness is also an integral part of this process. I carried a heavy load by taking on most of the parenting responsibilities. At times, I may have harbored bitterness and anger, which may have inadvertently affected our co-parenting relationship. I forgive myself for not always handling these emotions gracefully and instead commit to learning and growing from these experiences.

I strive to empathize with my co-parent's situation to embrace forgiveness fully. They may be facing personal or professional challenges that prevent them from being as involved as they would like. Forgiveness lets me momentarily step into their shoes and see things from their perspective without diminishing my experiences and feelings.

Moving forward, I must set realistic expectations for our co-parenting relationship. While I hope for their greater involvement, I cannot control their actions or decisions. I will focus on being my best parent for our children, providing them with love, support, and stability.

Forgiveness also means letting go of the fantasy of the "perfect" co-parenting arrangement. Accepting the reality of the situation allows me to find peace and make the most of the situation at hand. I will focus on nurturing a strong and positive bond with my children and creating a supportive environment for their growth and development.

As I walk the path of forgiveness, I strive to foster open communication with my co-parent. By expressing my feelings and concerns in a non-confrontational manner, we can work together more effectively for the well-being of our children. Finding common ground and establishing a united front in making important decisions concerning our children's lives is essential.

Forgiveness is not a one-time event but an ongoing process. There may be moments when I feel overwhelmed with emotions, which is normal. When those feelings arise, I will remind myself of the importance of forgiveness and its transformative power in releasing negative energy.

Forgiving my co-parent for their lack of involvement is a daily practice that requires compassion, self-awareness, and a commitment to growth. Through forgiveness, I can liberate myself from resentment and create a more positive co-parenting environment for our children. By focusing on the love and support I can provide, I take charge of my parenting journey and lay the foundation for a brighter future for our family.

Harmonious Meditative Thought of the Day

Today, I contemplate forgiving a co-parent's lack of involvement. It's an endeavor into compassion and understanding, recognizing that everyone has struggles and limitations.

Forgiveness in this context doesn't negate the challenges caused by their absence but liberates my heart from bitterness. It's a choice to release the weight of disappointment and redirect my energy towards nurturing a harmonious environment for my children.

In forgiving, I grant myself the gift of peace. I acknowledge that while their involvement may be lacking, my love and commitment to my children remain steadfast. It's about embracing the responsibility and privilege of providing a loving and supportive environment despite the circumstances.

As I forgive, I create space for healing and resilience, fostering a harmonious co-parenting dynamic that prioritizes the well-being of our children above all else. Today, I choose forgiveness as a path toward harmony and growth.

Deeper Connection Within

I forgive myself for judging _____
for the way they left me to _____
_____
_____.

I forgive myself for believing _____
should not _____
our children.

I forgive myself for my role in _____
_____
during our relationship.

Loving Statements About Me

I am embracing the healing power of forgiveness.

Their actions do not define me; my response defines me.

I am cultivating a peaceful heart and mind.

Gratitude Reflection of the Day

I'm grateful for the profound lessons in patience and empathy that co-parenting has taught me, fostering a deeper sense of self-love and compassion.

Inner Reflections

_____

_____

_____

_____

_____

_____

_____

_____

_____

_____

_____

_____

_____

_____

_____

_____

_____

_____

_____

I Forgive You For Rejecting Our Family

Forgiveness Reflection of the Day

Today, I embark on a daily reflection of forgiveness, focusing on the painful experience of my co-parent's rejection of our family. This journey has been arduous, filled with moments of heartache and confusion. Yet, I understand that forgiveness is not about excusing their actions but freeing myself from hurt and resentment.

When we started our co-parenting journey, I envisioned a united and supportive family environment for our children. However, as time passed, it became evident that my co-parent was emotionally distant and resistant to participating fully in our family dynamic. Their rejection felt like a deep and personal wound, leaving me with inadequacy and self-doubt.

Forgiving my co-parents begins with acknowledging their actions do not reflect my worth as a person or parent. Their rejection is not about me but likely stems from their unresolved issues, past experiences, or personal struggles. While this does not excuse their behavior, it helps me understand that their actions do not directly reflect my values or abilities.

Self-forgiveness is equally essential in this process. I must release the blame I placed on myself for their rejection. I forgive myself for the times I questioned my worth and the moments I allowed their actions to define me. I understand that I am worthy of love and acceptance, and their rejection does not define my worth as a parent or individual.

Empathy plays a vital role in forgiveness. I may uncover their reasons for the rejection by trying to understand my co-parent's perspective. They may be battling their emotional struggles, unable to fully engage in our family due to unresolved issues from their past. While their actions may have hurt me, practicing empathy helps me see their humanity beyond rejection.

Moving forward, I strive to establish healthy boundaries with my co-parent. Forgiveness doesn't mean forgetting the past; it means creating space for growth and change. I will prioritize my emotional well-being and set clear boundaries to protect myself and our children from further earm.

To embrace forgiveness fully, I aim to let go of the need for their approval or validation. I no longer want to be defined by their acceptance or rejection. Instead, I will focus on nurturing a supportive and loving environment for our children, surrounded by the people who cherish and appreciate our family.

As I walk this path of forgiveness, I commit to effective communication with my co-parent. While their rejection has caused pain, I recognize that open and honest dialogue is essential for the well-being of our children. Communicating my feelings in a constructive and non-confrontational manner might help them understand the impact of their actions.

I also focus on gratitude and appreciation for the positive aspects of our co-parenting relationship. While their rejection has been hurtful, there may still be moments of support and cooperation that I can acknowledge and cherish.

Forgiveness is a journey of healing and growth that requires patience and self-compassion. It is a choice I make every day, reminding myself that releasing the weight of resentment is liberating and empowering. It is an act of self-love and a gift to my children, who deserve to grow up in an environment free from the toxicity of unforgiveness.

Forgiving my co-parents for their rejection of our family is an ongoing process that involves understanding, empathy, and setting healthy boundaries. Through forgiveness, I release the emotional burden of their rejection, rediscovering my worth as a parent and individual. I focus on creating a positive and nurturing environment for our children, surrounded by love, acceptance, and the freedom to be who they are.

Harmonious Meditative Thought of the Day

Today, I embark on the transformative journey of forgiving my co-parent for rejecting our family. It's a path of profound healing and self-compassion. Forgiveness in this context doesn't mean dismissing the pain of rejection but releasing its grip on my heart.

By forgiving, I free myself from the heavy burden of resentment, making space for inner peace. It's an acknowledgment that each person's journey is complex, and their struggles and perspectives influence their choices.

Through forgiveness, I find the strength to focus on building a harmonious and loving environment for my family, even in the face of rejection. It's a choice to prioritize the well-being of those I cherish.

Today, I choose forgiveness to create harmony within myself and my family. It's a decisive step towards healing and resilience, a testament to the strength of love in the face of adversity.

Deeper Connection Within

I forgive myself for judging _____
_____ for the way they _____
_____
_____.

I forgive my mind for thinking _____
_____ presence was the only way our
family would be _____
_____.

I forgive my mind for thinking _____
will never _____
_____
for our children.

Loving Statements About Me

Every day, I am closer to complete healing and
forgiveness.

I release the past and create space for love and
positivity.

I am worthy of happiness, free from the shackles of
resentment.

Gratitude Reflection of the Day

I appreciate the support and understanding I've
received from loved ones and friends on this
co-parenting journey, knowing that their presence has
been a source of strength.

Inner Reflections

_____

_____

_____

_____

_____

_____

_____

_____

_____

_____

_____

_____

_____

_____

_____

_____

_____

_____

_____

I Forgive You For Prioritizing Other People Over Our Children

Forgiveness Reflection of the Day

Today, I embark on a daily reflection of forgiveness, seeking to understand and release the pain caused by my co-parent's prioritization of other things over our children. This journey has been emotionally taxing, leading me to question their commitment to our family's well-being. However, I understand that forgiveness is an act of compassion that can bring healing and growth to all involved.

Reflecting on my co-parent's choices, I recognize that life is complex, and each person navigates their responsibilities and priorities differently. While their decisions may have caused feelings of neglect or disappointment, I must remember that we are all human and sometimes face difficult life choices.

Forgiveness does not mean forgetting or condoning the impact of my co-parent's choices; instead, it allows me to release the grip of resentment and find a place of peace within myself. By forgiving, I am granting myself emotional freedom and paving the way for healthier co-parenting dynamics.

Self-forgiveness plays a crucial role in this journey. I release any blame I place on myself for being unable to control or change my priorities. I acknowledge that I cannot dictate their choices or force them to prioritize our children over other aspects of their lives. Instead, I focus on accepting that their actions are beyond my control and that my worth as a parent remains unchanged.

To truly embrace forgiveness, I attempt to understand my co-parent's perspective and the reasons behind their choices. They may grapple with personal challenges or face external pressures that influence their decisions. By seeking to empathize, I can humanize their actions and move away from feelings of anger or judgment.

Moving forward, I will focus on nurturing open communication with my co-parent. Effective dialogue can lead to a better understanding of each other's priorities and facilitate finding common ground in decisions related to our children. By fostering a collaborative co-parenting environment, we can work together to ensure our children's well-being remains a shared concern.

Setting healthy boundaries is essential in the forgiveness process. By establishing clear expectations and limitations regarding our children's needs, I can protect them from feeling neglected or emotionally burdened by our co-parent's choices. Healthy boundaries also enable me to prioritize my children's emotional well-being without compromising my own.

Gratitude plays a significant role in my journey of forgiveness. Instead of dwelling on my co-parent's shortcomings, I will focus on the positive aspects of our co-parenting relationship. I express gratitude for the times when they were present and involved in our children's lives, acknowledging that their inconsistent efforts are still valuable.

I relinquish the need for my co-parent's validation or approval through forgiveness. I recognize that their choices do not define my parenting abilities or worth. I am committed to being the best parent I can be, loving and supporting our children unconditionally.

This journey of forgiveness is not linear. There may be moments when I falter or revisit old feelings of hurt. During those times, I will be patient with myself and practice self-compassion. I will remind myself that forgiveness is a process and taking small steps toward healing. is okay

Forgiving my co-parent for prioritizing other things over our children is a journey of compassion, empathy, and understanding. I acknowledge their humanity and the complexities they face in life. Through forgiveness, I release resentment and prioritize my children's well-being. I strive to create a supportive and nurturing environment for them, filled with love, understanding, and emotional stability. By focusing on forgiveness, I move toward a brighter future, allowing myself to grow and heal.

Harmonious Meditative Thought of the Day

Today, I embrace the profound act of forgiving my co-parent for prioritizing others over our children. Forgiveness, in this context, is an act of compassion and understanding.

It acknowledges that people's choices are influenced by many factors, including their journey and challenges. While feeling hurt and protective of our children is natural, forgiveness frees our hearts from treatment.

Through forgiveness, I redirect my energy toward nurturing a harmonious environment for our children. It's about creating a loving and supportive space for them, regardless of external circumstances.

As I forgive, I empower myself to provide unwavering support and love for my children. It's a path toward harmony, where their well-being presents past grievances.

Today, I choose forgiveness to create a more harmonious and loving family dynamic for our children's sake.

Deeper Connection Within

I forgive my mind for believing _____
_____ prioritized _____

_____
_____ over our children.

I forgive my thoughts for judging _____
_____ when _____

_____
_____.

I forgive my mind for believing that my co-parent ____
_____
_____
_____.

Loving Statements About Me

I let go of pain and make room for joy in my heart.

Forgiveness is my gift to myself, and I give it willingly.

I am growing more robust through the process of forgiveness.

Gratitude Reflection of the Day

Today, I send kind and thankful thoughts to my co-parent, acknowledging the unique contributions and efforts they bring to our shared responsibility.

Inner Reflections

I Forgive You For The
Inconsistent Parenting

Forgiveness Reflection of the Day

Today's daily reflection centers on the journey of forgiving my co-parent for their inconsistencies in parenting. This process has been challenging as their unpredictable behavior often left me frustrated and uncertain. However, I recognize that forgiveness is essential in healing and fostering a more stable co-parenting environment.

As I reflect on my co-parent's inconsistent parenting, I remind myself that they, too, are human and prone to imperfections. Their actions may stem from their struggles, past experiences, or difficulties navigating parenting responsibilities. While this understanding doesn't excuse their behavior, it allows me to see them with empathy and compassion.

Forgiving my co-parent involves recognizing my role in this dynamic as well. There were times when I may have reacted to their inconsistencies with anger or resentment, adding to the tension between us. I must forgive myself for not always handling these emotions gracefully and commit to responding with patience and understanding moving forward.

To fully embrace forgiveness, I strive to communicate openly with my co-parent. Engaging in constructive conversations about their inconsistencies allows us to address concerns and explore potential solutions together. By approaching these discussions with empathy and a willingness to listen, we may uncover underlying issues and find common ground.

Self-forgiveness is equally vital in this process. I must release any self-blame for being unable to control my co-parent's behavior. It is not my responsibility to change them; instead, I can focus on adapting my reactions and actions to create a healthier co-parenting environment for our children.

Moving forward, I will work on setting clear and consistent boundaries for co-parenting. Establishing guidelines and expectations can help create stability for our children, regardless of the inconsistencies they may experience with the other parent. By maintaining consistency in my parenting approach, I provide a stable anchor for our children during times of uncertainty.

Gratitude is a powerful tool in forgiveness. Instead of dwelling on my co-parent's shortcomings, I focus on their positive contributions and efforts. Expressing gratitude for their presence and engagement in our children's lives can foster a more harmonious co-parenting relationship.

Forgiveness also means letting go of unrealistic expectations. Accepting that my co-parents do not always meet the standards I set for them as a parent allows me to find peace within myself. I must learn to accept them for who they are while prioritizing our children's well-being.

Through this journey of forgiveness, I am learning to release the need for validation from my co-parent. Their inconsistencies do not define my worth as a parent or diminish my love and dedication to our children. Despite the challenges we may face in co-parenting, I am committed to being the best parent I can be,

This process of forgiveness is not a one-time event but an ongoing practice. There may be moments when I find myself revisiting old feelings of frustration, but I am committed to staying on this path of growth and healing. Forgiveness requires patience with myself and a willingness to extend compassion to both my co-parent and myself.

Forgiving my co-parent for their inconsistencies in parenting is a journey of empathy, self-reflection, and acceptance. Through forgiveness, I let go of resentment and create space for healing. I focus on nurturing a stable and loving co-parenting environment for our children, filled with understanding, open communication, and unwavering support. By embracing forgiveness, I take charge of my emotional well-being and work towards a more positive co-parenting journey.

Harmonious Meditative Thought of the Day

Today, I find solace in forgiving my co-parent's inconsistencies in parenting. It's a journey toward harmony and understanding, recognizing that each of us brings unique strengths and challenges.

Inconsistencies may have caused confusion or frustration, but forgiveness allows me to release the weight of resentment. It's an act of self-compassion, acknowledging that parenting is a complex and ever-evolving journey.

Through forgiveness, I create space for open communication and collaboration. It's about embracing the imperfections and finding common ground for the well-being of our children.

As I forgive, I choose to provide stability and support for my children, providing a harmonious environment that values their needs above all else. Today, I let go of grievances and choose the path of forgiveness, fostering a more harmonious co-parenting dynamic for our children's growth and happiness.

Deeper Connection Within

I forgive myself for judging _____
for not _____
_____
_____ with our children.

I forgive myself for feeling _____
_____.

When the co-parent did not keep their word about ____
_____
_____
_____.

I forgive my mind for thinking _____
_____ will always _____
_____
_____.

Loving Statements About Me

I choose to focus on my growth and well-being.

My inner strength guides me toward healing and forgiveness.

I am free to create my narrative and release the past.

Gratitude Reflection of the Day

I'm thankful for the times when I've been able to set aside differences and prioritize the best interests of our children, fostering a sense of unity and cooperation.

Inner Reflections

_____

_____

_____

_____

_____

_____

_____

_____

_____

_____

_____

_____

_____

_____

_____

_____

_____

_____

I Forgive You For Breaking Promises To Our Children

Forgiveness Reflection of the Day

Today's daily reflection centers on forgiving your co-parent for breaking promises to your children. This process has been emotionally taxing, as their actions have caused disappointment and hurt in our family. However, I understand that forgiveness is a powerful tool that can bring healing and allow you to move forward more constructively.

Reflecting on my co-parent's broken promises, I remind myself that we are all human and prone to making mistakes. While their actions may have caused pain to our children, I acknowledge that they, too, are navigating their challenges and struggles. Forgiveness does not mean excusing their behavior, but it allows me to release the grip of anger and resentment, finding compassion for both my co-parent and myself.

I strive to empathize with my co-parent's perspective to embrace forgiveness fully. They may have made promises with good intentions, but unforeseen circumstances may have prevented them from fulfilling them. I try to put myself in their shoes and understand the complexities of balancing their responsibilities and commitments.

Self-forgiveness is equally vital in the process. I release any self-blame for being unable to control my co-parent's actions or protect our children from disappointment. I remind myself that I cannot shield our children from every hurtful experience, but Ian offers them love, support, and understanding during these challenging moments.

Moving forward, I will work on fostering open communication with my co-parent. Effective dialogue can help us address the impact of broken promises on our children and find solutions to avoid similar situations in the future. By communicating our expectations and limitations, we can collaborate to create a more reliable co-parenting environment.

Gratitude plays a significant role in my journey of forgiveness. Instead of dwelling on my co-parent's shortcomings, I focus on their positive contributions and efforts. Expressing gratitude for their presence and involvement in our children's lives can foster a more harmonious co-parenting relationship.

Forgiveness also means letting go of the need for their promises to validate my co-parenting efforts. Their broken promises do not diminish my dedication or love for our children. I focus on being a consistent and reliable parent, providing our children with stability and emotional support regardless of external circumstances.

Through this journey of forgiveness, I am learning to release the need for perfection. Accepting that my co-parent, like myself, is imperfect allows me to find peace within myself. I strive to embrace the reality that broken promises are growth opportunities, teaching our children resilience and the importance of forgiveness.

This process of forgiveness is not a one-time event but an ongoing practice. There may be moments when I find myself revisiting old feelings of disappointment and hurt, but I am committed to staying on this path of growth and healing. Forgiveness requires patience with myself and a willingness to extend compassion to both my co-parent and myself.

Forgiving my co-parent for breaking promises to our children is a journey of empathy, understanding, and acceptance. Through forgiveness, I let go of resentment and create space for healing. I focus on nurturing a supportive and loving co-parenting environment for our children, filled with communication, reliability, and unwavering love. By embracing forgiveness, I take charge of my emotional well-being and work towards a more positive co-parenting journey.

Harmonious Meditative Thought of the Day

Today, I embark on the path of forgiveness, extending compassion to my co-parent for breaking promises to our children. Forgiveness is a powerful act of grace that acknowledges life's complexities.

Promises broken may have caused disappointment and hurt, but forgiveness allows me to release the grip of resentment. It's an act of self-compassion, recognizing that no one is infallible.

Through forgiveness, I create a space for healing and communication. It's an opportunity to address our children's feelings and reassure them of our unwavering love.

As I forgive, I choose to be a steadfast source of support and stability for our children. It's a step towards harmony, where their emotional well-being presents past grievances.

Today, I embrace forgiveness to cultivate a harmonious co-parenting dynamic that values our children's happiness above all else.

Deeper Connection Within

I forgive my mind for judging _____
when they _____.

I forgive myself for judging _____ about
_____.

I forgive my mind for thinking I was responsible
for _____'s behavior and was
required to _____
_____when our children felt
let down.

Loving Statements About Me

I forgive, not because they deserve it, but because I
deserve peace.

My heart is a garden of forgiveness, nurturing love,
and understanding.

I release the grip of bitterness and welcome in
compassion.

Gratitude Reflection of the Day

I celebrate the moments of laughter and joy with
my children, which remind me of the importance of
cherishing every precious moment.

Inner Reflections

I Forgive Myself For Accepting The Disrespect For The " Sake of Peace"

Forgiveness Reflection of the Day

Today, as I reflect daily, I focus on the journey of forgiving myself for accepting disrespect from a co-parent to "keep the peace." This introspective process allows me to confront my actions, emotions, and motivations, ultimately paving the way toward healing and personal growth.

Looking back, I realize that my decision to tolerate disrespect from my co-parent stemmed from a deep desire to avoid conflict. I convinced myself that by staying silent and letting things slide, I was maintaining harmony for the sake of our shared responsibilities and the well-being of our children. However, this choice was expensive – my self-respect and emotional well-being.

Forgiving myself begins with acknowledging the complexity of the situation. I recognize that my intention was not to devalue myself or compromise my self-worth but to ensure a stable environment for our children. While my actions may not have aligned with my values, I was navigating a challenging co-parenting dynamic the best way I knew how.

Understanding the psychological dynamics that drove my decision to accept disrespect allows me to cultivate empathy toward myself. I remember that I was balancing multiple responsibilities and emotions, often feeling overwhelmed by the prospect of confrontation. Forgiveness requires me to recognize my vulnerability and treat myself with the same compassion I extend to others.

Self-forgiveness is also about releasing the burden of guilt. I acknowledge that I am not perfect and that making mistakes is a part of being human. Rather than dwelling on past decisions, I learn from them and consciously try to evolve and grow.

To fully embrace forgiveness, I challenge the limiting beliefs that led me to accept disrespect. I remind myself that maintaining peace does not require compromising my self-respect or tolerating mistreatment. I deserve to be treated with dignity and respect in all interactions, and I have the right to assert my boundaries healthily and assertively.

To forgive myself, I must also address the underlying fear that fueled my actions. The fear of conflict and its potential consequences significantly influenced my choices. By acknowledging this fear and its impact, I can work on building emotional resilience and practical communication skills that empower me to address challenges directly.

I commit to setting healthy boundaries and advocating for my self-worth. Forgiving myself means taking proactive steps to ensure I do not compromise my integrity in pursuing peace. I will prioritize open and respectful communication with my co-parent, seeking a resolution without sacrificing my self-esteem.

Reflecting on this journey of forgiveness, I understand that self-love is paramount. Forgiveness is an act of self-compassion, recognizing my inherent worthiness and valuing my emotional and mental well-being. By forgiving myself for accepting disrespect, I free myself from the weight of past decisions and create space for personal growth and empowerment.

Forgiving myself for accepting disrespect from a co-parent to "keep the peace" is a process of self-discovery, empathy, and growth. Through forgiveness, I release the grip of guilt and acknowledge my capacity for change. I commit to respecting my boundaries and nurturing a co-parenting dynamic built on mutual respect and understanding. By embracing forgiveness, I empower myself to create a more authentic and fulfilling co-parenting journey.

Harmonious Meditative Thought of the Day

Today, I embark on a journey of self-forgiveness, recognizing that I sometimes choose to overlook disrespect for the sake of peace. Forgiving myself is an act of compassion and growth.

In seeking harmony, I may have allowed boundaries to blur and my self-respect to wane. Forgiving myself means acknowledging that I, too, am a work in progress.

Through self-forgiveness, I create space for growth and self-improvement. It's an opportunity to learn from past choices and set healthier boundaries.

I commit to a harmonious relationship with my well-being as I forgive myself. It's about balancing peace and self-respect, ensuring that both are nurtured.

Today, I choose self-forgiveness to cultivate inner harmony, recognizing that my journey toward self-love and self-care is a continuous, evolving path.

Deeper Connection Within

I forgive myself for allowing _____
_____ to _____

_____
_____.

I forgive myself for judging my actions when I _____
_____
_____
_____.

I forgive my mind for believing I had to _____
_____
_____ to keep peace.

Loving Statements About Me

I am rewriting my story with forgiveness as the central theme.

I am creating a harmonious co-parenting dynamic through forgiveness.

I am taking back my power by letting go of resentment.

Gratitude Reflection of the Day

Today, I am filled with gratitude for the opportunity to co-parent, a role that continually challenges me to grow, evolve, and love unconditionally.

Inner Reflections

I Forgive You For Constantly Introducing Our Child To New Love Interests

Forgiveness Reflection of the Day

In the tapestry of co-parenting, forgiveness has become a powerful thread woven through the complex emotions I've experienced. The challenge I've faced in forgiving my co-parent for repeatedly introducing our children to new girlfriends has been a profound journey of growth, understanding, and healing.

At the outset, I admit that this situation stirred emotions. Each new introduction felt like a disruption to the stability I sought to provide for our children. Questions and concerns filled my thoughts: Were our children confused or insecure? How would these experiences shape their understanding of relationships and commitment? Yet, as I journey through forgiveness, I recognize that my co-parent's actions stem from their life choices, not necessarily a lack of consideration for our children's well-being.

Forgiving my co-parent starts with acknowledging the complexity of adult relationships and personal choices. In searching for companionship and happiness, they may pursue their path toward fulfillment. While these introductions affect our children's lives, separating their actions from their intentions is essential, allowing room for empathy and understanding.

I also realize the importance of forgiving myself in this process. It's easy to fall into the trap of self-blame, questioning my decisions and emotions. However, I understand that my valid reactions do not define my worth as a parent or my ability to provide a nurturing environment. Self-forgiveness involves letting go of guilt and embracing the truth that I am doing my best in a complex situation.

To fully embrace forgiveness, I strive to put myself in my co-parent's shoes. I attempt to understand the reasons behind their actions, acknowledging that their choices may arise from their desires for companionship and love. While their intentions might not align with my preferences, forgiveness lets me step away from judgment and cultivate empathy.

Moving forward, I commit to open communication with my co-parent. By expressing my concerns constructively and respectfully, I aim to establish a shared understanding of the potential impact of these introductions on our children. Engaging in honest conversations can lay the foundation for a co-parenting dynamic that prioritizes the well-being of our children.

Forgiveness also entails letting go of the need to control the co-parent's choices. While I hold a shared responsibility for our children's lives, I must acknowledge that I cannot dictate the direction of my co-parent's relationships. Letting go of this need for control allows me to focus on what I can directly influence: my relationship with my children and the environment I provide for them.

As I reflect on this journey of forgiveness, I am reminded that forgiveness is not a single, isolated act but an ongoing practice. There may be moments when I feel the sting of frustration or concern, but through forgiveness, I can transform these emotions into a source of strength and resilience.

Forgiving my co-parent for introducing our children to new girlfriends is a process of understanding, empathy, and growth. Through forgiveness, I free myself from resentment and focus on creating a positive and nurturing co-parenting environment. By extending forgiveness to myself and my co-parent, I demonstrate to our children the value of compassion, empathy, and emotional resilience. In doing so, I contribute to their well-being and ability to navigate human relationships' complexities.

Harmonious Meditative Thought of the Day

Today, I embark on the path of forgiveness, extending understanding to my co-parent for constantly introducing our children to new girlfriends. Forgiveness is an act of compassion, recognizing that everyone's choices are influenced by their journey.

The constant introduction of new partners may have caused confusion or concern, but forgiveness allows me to release the weight of resentment. It's an act of self-compassion, acknowledging the complexities of co-parenting.

Through forgiveness, I create space for open communication and cooperation. It's an opportunity to discuss our children's feelings and ensure a stable, nurturing environment.

As I forgive, I choose to be a constant source of love and support for our children. It's a step towards harmony, where their emotional well-being precedes past grievances.

Today, I embrace forgiveness to cultivate a more harmonious co-parenting dynamic that prioritizes our children's sense of stability and security.

Deeper Connection Within

I forgive my mind for judging _____
_____ when _____
_____
_____.

I forgive myself for believing _____
_____ should not _____
_____
with our children.

I forgive myself for believing _____
_____ will _____
_____ our children by
introducing them to _____.

Loving Statements About Me

My heart is open, and I am willing to heal and grow.

Forgiveness is a balm that soothes my wounded soul.

I am forgiving, not for them, but for my inner peace.

Gratitude Reflection of the Day

I appreciate the wisdom and insight I've gained through co-parenting, knowing that it has enriched my understanding of myself and the complexities of family dynamics.

Inner Reflections

I Forgive You For Always Leaving Our Children With Your Parents

Forgiveness Reflection of the Day

In the intricate tapestry of co-parenting, forgiveness has been an essential thread woven through the complex emotions I've experienced. Today, I find myself reflecting on the journey of forgiving my co-parent for consistently leaving our children in the care of their parents instead of spending quality time with them. This journey has been marked by a range of emotions – disappointment, frustration, and sadness – yet it holds the potential for growth, healing, and understanding.

As I navigate the landscape of forgiveness, I realize that my co-parent's actions may stem from their unique circumstances and struggles. While their choices may have left our children yearning for their presence, I am learning to differentiate between their actions and intentions. By doing so, I am cultivating a space for empathy and compassion, allowing me to let go of resentment and its weight.

Forgiving my co-parent also involves extending that same compassion towards myself. It's natural to question whether I could have done more to influence their decisions or to provide a different perspective. However, I recognize that I can only control my actions and reactions. Self-forgiveness requires letting go of self-blame and acknowledging that I, too, am navigating the complexities of co-parenting to the best of my ability.

To fully embrace forgiveness, I try to see the situation from my co-parent's perspective. They may be grappling with work, personal, or emotional challenges that influence their decisions. While it doesn't justify their absence, it helps me understand the broader context in which their choices are made.

Moving forward, I commit to fostering open communication with my co-parent. By expressing my concerns and feelings in a non-confrontational manner, we can create an environment that encourages honest dialogue about our children's needs. Communicating my observations and discussing the impact of their actions on our children can lead to a shared understanding and drive positive change.

Forgiveness also requires letting go of the need for control. While I hold shared responsibility for our children's well-being, I understand that I cannot control my co-parent's choices or actions. Letting go of this need for control empowers me to focus on providing a stable and supportive environment for our children within my sphere of influence.

As I reflect on this journey of forgiveness, I am reminded that forgiveness is not an isolated act but a continuous practice. There may be moments when I find myself revisiting feelings of disappointment or frustration, but through forgiveness, I can transform these emotions into a catalyst for growth and understanding.

In conclusion, forgiving my co-parent for consistently leaving our children in the care of their parents is a journey marked by empathy, self-compassion, and growth. Through forgiveness, I release the grip of resentment and create space for healing. I am fostering a co-parenting environment rooted in understanding, empathy, and love by extending forgiveness to my co-parent and myself. In doing so, I am prioritizing the emotional well-being of our children and contributing to their ability to navigate complex relationships with compassion and resilience in the future.

Harmonious Meditative Thought of the Day

Today, I embark on a profound journey of forgiveness, extending understanding to my co-parent for consistently leaving our children with their parents. Forgiveness is an act of compassion that acknowledges the complexities of life.

The consistent pattern of leaving our children with their grandparents may have stirred feelings of frustration or concern, but forgiveness empowers me to release the grip of resentment. It's an act of self-compassion, recognizing that parenting is a complex balancing act.

Through forgiveness, I create space for open dialogue and cooperation. It's an opportunity to discuss our children's needs and concerns, ensuring their well-being is a shared priority.

As I forgive, I choose to be a steady source of love and support for our children, promoting harmony and understanding. Today, I embrace forgiveness to foster a more harmonious co-parenting dynamic that values our children's happiness and security above all else.

Deeper Connection Within

I forgive myself for believing _____
_____ should _____

_____
_____.

I forgive myself for judging _____
when they _____

_____
_____.

I forgive my mind for thinking _____
_____ should not _____

_____
_____.

Loving Statements About Me

I am capable of rising above any challenges and finding forgiveness.

I am choosing forgiveness as a path to a brighter future.

I am honoring my journey by embracing forgiveness.

Gratitude Reflection of the Day

I'm grateful for the strength and resilience I've developed as a co-parent, recognizing that I am capable of navigating challenges with grace and determination.

Inner Reflections

I Forgive You For Avoiding Your Financial Responsibility For Our Children

Forgiveness Reflection of the Day

In the intricate dance of co-parenting, I find myself reflecting on the challenges posed by a co-parent who refuses to contribute financially to the upbringing of our children. This journey of navigating co-parenting amidst financial disparities has tested my patience, resilience, and ability to balance my children's well-being and emotional and financial stability.

As I embark on this reflection, I recognize the importance of forgiveness – not only towards my co-parent but also towards myself. I acknowledge that the situation I find myself in is complex, and it is easy to succumb to feelings of frustration, anger, or helplessness. However, forgiveness empowers me to let go of these negative emotions and focus on finding productive solutions.

Forgiving my co-parent begins with understanding that their refusal to contribute financially may stem from their circumstances and struggles. While their actions may impact our children's well-being, I strive to separate their choices from their intentions. This perspective allows me to approach the situation with empathy and compassion, fostering an environment conducive to open communication.

Moreover, I extend self-forgiveness to myself. It is natural to question whether I am doing enough or should be able to influence their choices. However, self-forgiveness requires releasing guilt and acknowledging that I am doing my best in a challenging situation.

To fully embrace forgiveness, I strive to communicate honestly and openly with my co-parent. By addressing the issue calmly and assertively, I create an opportunity for us to discuss the importance of financial contributions for the well-being of our children. While this conversation may yield little results, it sets the stage for future dialogue and potential cooperation.

I also acknowledge the importance of seeking support from legal and professional channels when necessary. While forgiveness is a powerful tool for emotional healing, practical steps may need to be taken to ensure the financial stability of my children. Seeking legal advice or mediation can provide a framework for negotiating financial responsibilities.

Moving forward, I focus on empowerment. While I cannot control my co-parent's choices, I can control how I respond and take charge of my children's financial well-being. This empowerment involves exploring potential resources, such as government assistance programs or community support, to provide my family with a safety net.

Forgiveness also means letting go of relying solely on my co-parent. While their financial contributions are essential, I can provide emotional and financial stability for my children on my terms. By fostering my resilience and resourcefulness, I demonstrate to my children the importance of facing challenges head-on and finding solutions.

Through this journey of forgiveness, I am reminded that forgiveness is an ongoing practice. There may be moments when frustration or resentment resurface, but I can transform these emotions into a source of strength and determination through forgiveness.

Navigating co-parenting when faced with a co-parent who refuses to help financially is a journey marked by empathy, empowerment, and practicality. Through forgiveness, I release the grip of negative emotions and create space for healing. By extending forgiveness to both my co-parent and myself, I am fostering an environment focused on the well-being and stability of our children. In doing so, I nurture their resilience and teach them valuable life lessons about facing challenges and finding strength in adversity.

Harmonious Meditative Thought of the Day

Today, I embark on a transformative journey of forgiveness, extending understanding to my co-parent for avoiding their financial responsibility for our children. Forgiveness is an act of grace and empathy, recognizing the complexity of financial challenges.

Avoiding financial responsibility may have caused stress and frustration, but forgiveness empowers me to release the grip of resentment. It's an act of self-compassion, understanding that life's circumstances can be overwhelming.

Through forgiveness, I create space for open communication and cooperation. It's an opportunity to discuss our children's needs and ensure their well-being remains a shared commitment.

As I forgive, I choose to be a resilient pillar of support for our children, prioritizing their emotional and financial stability. Today, I embrace forgiveness to foster a more harmonious co-parenting dynamic that places our children's welfare at the forefront of our shared responsibilities.

Deeper Connection Within

I forgive myself for judging _____
for _____
_____
_____.

I forgive my mind for believing if _____
did not _____
_____
it would _____
_____
_____.

I forgive my thought for believing _____
_____ will never _____
_____
_____ for our children.

Loving Statements About Me

My heart is expanding with love and understanding.

I am unburdening myself by releasing old grudges.

I am reclaiming my energy by letting go of resentment.

Gratitude Reflection of the Day

Today, I recognize the beauty of self-love as a foundation for effective co-parenting, allowing me to extend love, patience, and understanding to my children and their other parent.

Inner Reflections

I Forgive Myself For Co-Parenting While Being Emotionally Bankrupt

Forgiveness Reflection of the Day

As I take a moment to reflect on my journey of parenting while feeling emotionally bankrupt, I am met with a complex tapestry of emotions, challenges, and personal growth. This journey has demanded unwavering strength, self-compassion, and a deep commitment to the well-being of my children.

At times, the weight of emotional exhaustion has felt overwhelming. The demands of daily life, personal struggles, and parenting responsibilities have converged, leaving me feeling drained and depleted. There have been moments when I questioned my ability to provide the emotional support and stability my children deserve.

Through self-reflection, I acknowledge the importance of forgiveness towards myself and the circumstances I find myself in. It's easy to fall into the trap of self-blame, questioning whether I am doing enough or whether my emotional state is negatively impacting my children. However, forgiveness allows me to release guilt and recognize that I am doing my best in my circumstances.

I also recognize that seeking help is a sign of strength, not weakness. As a financially bankrupt individual might seek financial assistance, I can seek emotional support when needed. Whether confiding in a friend, seeking therapy, or participating in support groups, these actions are essential for my well-being and ultimately benefit my children.

To navigate parenting while emotionally bankrupt, I am learning to be honest with myself and my children. Open communication, even about my emotional struggles, fosters a sense of trust and transparency. While I may not have many emotional resources, I can still provide a safe space for my children to express their feelings and share their concerns.

Self-care is an integral part of this journey. Just as an empty bank account requires responsible management, my emotional well-being requires nurturing and attention. I am learning to prioritize self-care routines that replenish my emotional reserves – engaging in hobbies, practicing mindfulness, or taking moments of solitude.

Forgiveness is also about relinquishing the pressure to be a perfect parent. Embracing my imperfections and acknowledging that I cannot always shield my children from my emotional struggles is a crucial step towards self-forgiveness. Through self-compassion, I can teach my children the importance of self-care and resilience in facing challenges.

Moving forward, I am committed to seeking moments of joy and connection with my children. While I may be emotionally bankrupt at times, I can still create meaningful memories and experiences that nurture our bond. Quality time together, filled with love and attention, can help offset the emotional challenges we may be facing.

In this journey of self-reflection, I am reminded that emotional bankruptcy does not define me as a parent. It is a temporary state that I am actively working to overcome. Through forgiveness, self-compassion, and seeking support, I am building a foundation of resilience and strength that will ultimately benefit me and my children.

Parenting while feeling emotionally bankrupt is a journey marked by self-reflection, growth, and determination. Through forgiveness, I release the weight of guilt and embrace the reality of my circumstances. By prioritizing self-care, seeking support, and fostering open communication, I demonstrate resilience and teach my children the value of facing challenges gracefully and compassionfully. This journey is a testament to the strength of the human spirit and our enduring love for our children.

Harmonious Meditative Thought of the Day

Today, I embark on a journey of self-forgiveness, extending compassion to myself for parenting when I was emotionally bankrupt. Forgiving myself is an act of profound self-compassion.

Parenting, while emotionally drained, may have left me feeling guilty or inadequate, but forgiveness allows me to release the weight of self-blame. It's an acknowledgment that, as a human, I have my limits.

Through self-forgiveness, I create space for healing and growth. It's an opportunity to learn from past experiences, seek support, and prioritize self-care.

As I forgive myself, I commit to being a more compassionate and understanding parent. It's about recognizing that self-care is not selfish but essential for providing the best care for my children.

Today, I choose self-forgiveness to cultivate inner harmony, knowing that my journey as a parent is one of continuous learning and self-improvement.

I forgive myself for parenting while being emotionally bankrupt.

Deeper Connection Within

I forgive myself for _____

_____ when I _____

_____

_____.

I forgive my mind for believing I always needed to ____

_____

_____

_____.

I forgive myself for thinking I could never _____

_____.

Loving Statements About Me

I am free to heal and grow beyond the pain of the past.

Forgiveness is a gift I give myself, and I receive it gratefully.

I am creating a legacy of love and healing for myself and my children.

Gratitude Reflection of the Day

I'm thankful for the moments of connection and bonding with my children, which fill our co-parenting journey with warmth and love.

Inner Reflections

(lined journal page for writing)

I Forgive My Mind For Believing You Didn't Truly Want Joint Custody...But Wanted...

Forgiveness Reflection of the Day

As I embark on a journey of self-reflection, I find myself grappling with the need to forgive my mind for passing judgment on a co-parent's intentions. The realization that their desire for joint custody might have been driven by a wish to avoid paying child support has stirred a mix of emotions within me – from frustration to disappointment. Yet, in this introspective journey, I recognize the transformative power of forgiveness and its potential to bring clarity, healing, and empathy.

Forgiving my judgments is an act of acknowledging my humanity. It is natural for the mind to make assumptions based on the information available. However, I am learning that these assumptions often need to be completed and accurately capture the complexity of another person's motivations and circumstances. Through forgiveness, I release the grip of judgment and create space for understanding and empathy.

In the process of forgiveness, I am also learning to practice self-compassion. I quickly blame myself for making conclusions or letting negative thoughts cloud my perception. However, self-compassion requires treating myself with the same kindness I would offer to a friend. I remind myself that I am a product of my experiences and that my judgments do not define my worth.

To fully embrace forgiveness, I strive to put myself in the co-parent's shoes. While their actions may not align with my expectations or desires, it is crucial to consider the broader context in which their decisions were made. They, too, may be navigating their challenges, fears, and uncertainties. I can shift from judgment to empathy by attempting to understand their perspective.

I commit to challenging my assumptions and engaging in open communication. I can gain deeper insights into their motivations and intentions by initiating a respectful and honest dialogue with the co-parent. This conversation clarifies their reasons for seeking joint custody and allows us to find common ground.

Forgiveness also means releasing the need for validation from the co-parent's actions. Their choices do not diminish my worth as a parent or my love and dedication for our children. By focusing on my commitment to providing a nurturing and supportive environment for our children, I can transcend the limitations of judgment and resentment.

In this journey of forgiveness, I am reminded that I am not alone in facing inner conflicts. The co-parent may also deal with their challenges and struggles as I work to forgive my judgments. Acknowledging our shared humanity, I pave the way for a more compassionate and harmonious co-parenting dynamic.

Forgiving my mind for passing judgment on a co-parent's intentions is a transformative journey of self-awareness, understanding, and growth. Through forgiveness, I let go of the weight of the decision and opened myself to the possibility of empathy and compassion. I am fostering an environment rooted in understanding, respect, and effective communication by extending forgiveness to myself and the co-parent. In doing so, I contribute to a more positive co-parenting relationship and create a healthier foundation for our children's well-being.

Harmonious Meditative Thought of the Day

Today, I embark on the path of forgiveness, extending compassion to my mind for judging a co-parent who pretended to want to spend time with our kids but had ulterior motives. Forgiveness is not only for others but also for ourselves, recognizing the complexity of human nature.

My initial judgment may have been a protective response, but forgiveness allows me to release the weight of resentment and self-judgment. It's an act of self-compassion, understanding that our minds are wired to make sense of the world.

Through forgiveness, I create space for a more open-hearted perspective. It's an opportunity to approach future situations with discernment and wisdom without the burden of past judgments.

As I forgive my mind, I cultivate a more harmonious and balanced mindset that promotes understanding and empathy. Today, I embrace forgiveness to foster inner peace and emotional resilience.

Deeper Connection Within

I forgive my mind for believing _____
_____ wanted to
_____
_____.

I forgive my mind for thinking _____
_____ did not _____
_____
_____.

I forgive myself for _____
_____ ─ ─ ─ ─
when _____
_____.

Loving Statements About Me

I deserve a life filled with joy, peace, and forgiveness.

My heart is lightening as I release the weight of unforgiveness.

I am nurturing my spirit through the act of forgiveness.

Gratitude Reflection of the Day

I appreciate the opportunity to model resilience and cooperation for my children, showing them the value of working together in challenging situations.

Inner Reflections

I Welcome Forgiveness' Energy To Heal From Your Hurtful Words

Forgiveness Reflection of the Day

As I embark on a journey of introspection, I reflect on the challenging path of forgiving a co-parent who has hurtfully bad-mouthing me to our children. This journey of forgiveness is an intricate process that involves navigating through various emotions, from pain and anger to understanding and healing.

Forgiving a co-parent for bad-mouthing me to our children is not an easy task, but I recognize that it is a necessary step for my well-being and the well-being of our children. To start this journey, I acknowledge that forgiveness does not mean excusing or justifying their behavior. It means releasing the emotional burden that comes with holding onto resentment and anger.

Understanding the source of their actions is an essential part of the forgiveness process. The co-parent's behavior may stem from their struggles, insecurities, or unresolved issues. While this doesn't excuse their actions, it offers a glimpse into the complexities of their emotions and motivations. By understanding their perspective, I can begin to let go of my negative emotions.

In forgiving a co-parent, I am also forgiving myself. It's natural to feel hurt and frustrated by their words, but I must remind myself that their actions do not define my worth as a parent or person. Self-forgiveness involves acknowledging that I am doing my best in a difficult situation and deserve love and respect from others.

I commit to fostering open communication with the co-parent to embrace forgiveness fully. I can express how their words have impacted me and our children by addressing the issue directly and calmly. This conversation may not immediately change their behavior, but sets the foundation for a healthier co-parenting dynamic.

Moving beyond forgiveness, I strive to create a positive and nurturing environment for our children. I want to ensure they feel safe and supported despite negative influences. By focusing on my actions and behavior as a parent, I can counteract the adverse effects of bad-mouthing and provide a strong foundation for our children's emotional well-being.

I also recognize the importance of setting boundaries. While forgiveness is essential, it doesn't mean I have to tolerate ongoing disrespectful behavior. Establishing clear limitations with the co-parent can help prevent further bad-mouthing and create a more respectful co-parenting relationship.

In this journey of forgiveness, I am reminded that healing takes time. It's natural to have moments when old hurt feelings resurface, but forgiveness allows me to transform them into opportunities for growth and healing. It's a gradual process that requires patience and self-compassion.

Forgiving a co-parent for bad-mouthing me to our children is a journey of understanding, self-compassion, and healing. Through forgiveness, I release resentment and create space for positive change. By extending forgiveness to both the co-parent and myself, I am fostering an environment of respect, open communication, and emotional well-being. In doing so, I am contributing to a healthier co-parenting relationship and ensuring our children are surrounded by love, support, and understanding.

Harmonious Meditative Thought of the Day

Today, I embark on a profound journey of forgiveness, extending understanding to my co-parents for their hurtful words to our children. Forgiveness is an act of compassion and healing, recognizing the complexity of emotions.

Hurtful words may have left scars, but forgiveness empowers me to release the grip of anger and resentment. It's an act of self-compassion, understanding that we can all make mistakes.

Through forgiveness, I create space for open communication and emotional growth. It's an opportunity to discuss the impact of hurtful words on our children and work together to heal those wounds.

As I forgive, I provide emotional support and understanding for our children, promoting harmony and emotional resilience. Today, I embrace forgiveness to foster a more harmonious co-parenting dynamic that values our children's emotional well-being above all else.

Deeper Connection Within

I forgive my mind for believing _____ always
_____.

I forgive myself for not _____
_____.

I forgive myself for judging _____
for _____.

Loving Statements About Me

I want to see the good during challenges.

I am letting go of the past and stepping into a brighter future.

I am rewriting the script of my co-parenting journey with forgiveness.

Gratitude Reflection of the Day

Today, I send loving energy to my co-parenting relationship, expressing my gratitude for the growth, understanding, and love that it continues to bring into my life.

Inner Reflections

_____

_____

_____

_____

_____

_____

_____

_____

_____

_____

_____

_____

_____

_____

_____

_____

_____

_____

_____

I Forgive You For Being A "Disneyland" Co-Parent

Forgiveness Reflection of the Day

In the complex tapestry of co-parenting, I find myself on a reflective journey towards forgiveness – forgiving a co-parent who has assumed the role of a "Disneyland" dad. This path of understanding requires me to navigate a range of emotions, from frustration to acceptance, as I come to terms with the impact of their parenting style on our children and our co-parenting dynamic.

As I embark on this journey, I recognize that forgiveness is not synonymous with condoning or excusing behavior. It is about liberating myself from resentment and finding a way to coexist that benefits our children and fosters a more harmonious co-parenting relationship.

Understanding the motivations behind the "Disneyland" dad persona is integral to forgiveness. While their approach may prioritize fun and indulgence, their intentions are rooted in a desire to create memorable experiences for our children. By attempting to empathize with their perspective, I can move beyond judgment and begin to forge a path toward healing.

In forgiving the co-parent, I also extend forgiveness to myself. It's natural to question my parenting choices and feel a sense of inadequacy in comparison to their seemingly exciting outings. However, self-forgiveness requires acknowledging that my parenting style is valuable and necessary. I am doing my best to provide our children with a stable and nurturing environment, which is equally essential.

To fully embrace forgiveness, I commit to open communication with the co-parent. By expressing my concerns and discussing the potential impact of their parenting approach on our children, we can work towards finding common ground. This conversation may lead to a deeper understanding of each other's perspectives and enable us to collaborate for the well-being of our children.

Moving forward, I aim to focus on the positives that the "Disneyland" dad brings to our children's lives. While their approach may differ from mine, it offers our children unique experiences and memories they cherish. By recognizing the value of our parenting styles, I can foster an environment that allows our children to thrive and grow.

Forgiveness also means letting go of the need to control or compete with the co-parent's approach. Instead of fixating on the differences, I can strengthen my connection with our children. By maintaining open lines of communication and fostering emotional closeness, I can ensure that my role as a parent remains influential and impactful.

In this journey of forgiveness, I am reminded that healing takes time. It's natural to have moments of frustration or doubt, but I can transform them into opportunities for growth and understanding through forgiveness. The journey is a gradual process that requires patience, empathy, and self-compassion.

Forgiving a co-parent for assuming the role of a "Disneyland" dad is a journey of empathy, self-compassion, and understanding. Through forgiveness, I release the grip of resentment and create space for positive change. By extending forgiveness to both the co-parent and myself, I am fostering an environment of collaboration, open communication, and emotional well-being. In doing so, I contribute to a healthier co-parenting relationship and ensure that our children benefit from the strengths of both parenting styles, ultimately growing into well-rounded individuals.

Harmonious Meditative Thought of the Day

Today, I embark on the transformative journey of forgiveness, extending understanding to my co-parent for being a "Disneyland" parent, showing up mainly for fun activities. Forgiveness is an act of empathy and healing, recognizing that parenting comes with its complexities.

This approach may have caused feelings of imbalance or frustration, but forgiveness empowers me to release the weight of judgment and resentment. It's an act of self-compassion, acknowledging that each co-parenting style has unique qualities.

Through forgiveness, I create space for open dialogue and cooperation. It's an opportunity to discuss our roles and ensure our children receive a balanced upbringing.

As I forgive, I choose to be a steadfast source of love and support for our children, offering them a stable and nurturing environment. Today, I embrace forgiveness to foster a more harmonious co-parenting dynamic that prioritizes our children's well-rounded development above all else.

Deeper Connection Within

I forgive my mind for believing _____
will never _____ for our
children.

I forgive myself for not _____
_____ when _____.

I forgive myself for judging _____
for not being _____.

Loving Statements About Me

I am choosing to rise above negativity and embrace positivity.

I am becoming a beacon of love, healing, and forgiveness.

My heart is a sanctuary of peace, free from resentment.

Gratitude Reflection of the Day

I'm thankful for the support and encouragement I receive from those who understand the complexities of co-parenting, knowing that their guidance is a valuable source of wisdom.

Inner Reflections

DAY 18

I Forgive Myself For Micro-Managing While Co-Parenting

Forgiveness Reflection of the Day

As I embark on a journey of self-reflection, I find myself exploring the intricate layers of forgiving myself for tendencies to micro-manage while co-parenting. This introspective process allows me to confront my actions, acknowledge their impact, and work towards a healthier co-parenting dynamic built on trust, respect, and personal growth.

Admitting the presence of micro-management in my co-parenting approach is the first step towards forgiveness. It's easy to succumb to the belief that my actions stem from a place of genuine concern. Yet, I recognize that excessive control may inadvertently undermine the co-parenting relationship and contribute to an unhealthy dynamic.

Forgiving myself involves understanding the underlying motivations behind my micro-management tendencies. My desire to ensure our children's well-being sometimes led me to overstep boundaries. While my intentions were rooted in love and protection, I understand that allowing the co-parent space to make decisions is equally essential for their growth and the children's sense of balance.

Self-forgiveness also entails acknowledging that I am human and prone to imperfections. It's natural to look back and question my choices, but dwelling on past mistakes only perpetuates negative feelings. Embracing self-compassion allows me to accept that growth involves recognizing areas for improvement and taking proactive steps toward change.

To fully embrace forgiveness, I commit to improving communication with the co-parent. Honest and open dialogue is critical to establishing mutual understanding and respect. By discussing our co-parenting goals, concerns, and expectations, we can find common ground and develop a unified approach that respects each other's autonomy.

Moving forward, I am determined to relinquish the need for constant control. Micro-managing restricts the co-parent's involvement and limits my ability to focus on nurturing a healthy relationship with our children. By relinquishing control and allowing the co-parent to take ownership of their decisions, I create space for them to contribute positively to our children's upbringing.

Forgiveness is also about fostering self-awareness. I am committed to recognizing triggers that prompt my micro-management tendencies and finding healthier ways to address them. This might involve seeking support from a therapist, engaging in mindfulness practices, or pursuing personal growth activities that help me manage anxiety or uncertainty.

In this journey of self-reflection, I am reminded that growth is a continuous process. Forgiveness doesn't erase the past but is a foundation for positive change moving forward. I understand it's okay to ask for help, learn from my mistakes, and evolve into a co-parent who empowers both myself and the co-parent to create a supportive and nurturing environment for our children.

Forgiving myself for micro-managing while co-parenting is a journey of self-discovery, understanding, and growth. Through forgiveness, I release the weight of guilt and open myself to the possibility of positive change. By extending forgiveness to myself and committing to healthier co-parenting practices, I am fostering an environment of collaboration, respect, and growth. In doing so, I contribute to a more balanced and harmonious co-parenting relationship that benefits myself and our children.

Harmonious Meditative Thought of the Day

Today, I embark on a path of self-forgiveness, extending compassion to myself for moments of micro-managing while co-parenting. Forgiveness is an act of self-compassion and growth.

Micro-managing may have arisen from a place of concern, but forgiveness allows me to release the weight of self-criticism and guilt. It's an acknowledgment that, as a co-parent, I am constantly learning and evolving.

Through self-forgiveness, I create space for personal growth and better communication. It's an opportunity to seek a balance between ensuring my child's well-being and allowing for the autonomy of my co-parent.

As I forgive myself, I commit to being a more patient, understanding, and harmonious co-parent. It's about recognizing that growth and learning are integral to co-parenting.

Today, I choose self-forgiveness to cultivate inner peace and foster a more harmonious co-parenting dynamic that values mutual respect and cooperation.

I welcome growth as I forgive myself for micro-managing and trying to control the way _____ co-parents.

Deeper Connection Within

I forgive my mind for believing _____ is not
_____.

I forgive myself for thinking _____
will always _____.

I forgive myself for judging _____
for _____.

Loving Statements About Me

I am forgiving, not for them, but for my well-being.

I am growing stronger every day as I embrace self-forgiveness.

I am taking control of my emotional well-being through forgiveness.

Gratitude Reflection of the Day

I celebrate the moments of clarity and insight that co-parenting has offered, guiding me toward greater self-awareness and self-acceptance.

Inner Reflections

I Forgive Myself For Lying To Our Children To Protect Your Image

Forgiveness Reflection of the Day

As I embark on a journey of self-reflection, I am confronted with the need to forgive myself for the times I chose to lie to our children to protect a co-parent's image. This introspective process prompts me to confront the complexities of co-parenting, the impact of my actions on our children, and the path toward personal growth and healing.

Admitting my choice to lie, even with good intentions, is a crucial step towards self-forgiveness. It's natural to want to shield our children from potential harm or discomfort, but I recognize that dishonesty can inadvertently undermine their trust in me and the co-parent. Acknowledging the consequences of my actions is an essential part of the forgiveness journey.

To forgive myself, I must understand the motivations that led me to lie. The desire to present a positive image of the co-parent may have been rooted in a genuine intention to preserve their relationship with our children. Yet, I also acknowledge that honesty and transparency are vital for nurturing a healthy co-parenting dynamic and fostering trust with our children.

Self-forgiveness entails accepting my imperfections and understanding that growth involves acknowledging mistakes. Instead of dwelling on the past, I focus on learning from my actions and making conscious choices to prioritize honesty and open communication moving forward. Self-compassion allows me to treat myself with kindness, acknowledging that I am capable of change and personal growth.

I prioritize open and honest communication with our children to fully embrace forgiveness. Creating an environment where they feel comfortable discussing their thoughts and emotions is crucial for their emotional well-being. By fostering a safe space for dialogue, I can address any questions or concerns they may have about our co-parenting relationship.

Moving forward, I strive to model authenticity and integrity for our children. By being truthful about my actions and experiences, I demonstrate the importance of honesty and accountability. This approach strengthens my bond with our children and encourages them to cultivate respectful and open relationships.

Forgiveness also involves letting go of the need to protect the co-parent's image at all costs. While it's essential to promote a positive co-parenting relationship, it shouldn't come at the expense of sacrificing my integrity or the well-being of our children. Balancing the co-parent's image with the truth allows for a more authentic and sustainable co-parenting dynamic.

In this journey of self-reflection, I am reminded that personal growth is a continuous process. Forgiveness catalyzes positive change, urging me to continually reassess my actions and make intentional choices aligned with my values. It's a reminder that I can evolve into a co-parent who prioritizes honesty, respect, and emotional well-being.

In conclusion, forgiving myself for lying to our children to protect a co-parent's image is a journey of self-discovery, growth, and accountability. Through forgiveness, I release the weight of guilt and open myself to the potential for positive change. By extending forgiveness to myself and committing to a path of honesty and open communication, I am fostering an environment of trust, authenticity, and personal development. In doing so, I contribute to a co-parenting relationship that values our children's emotional well-being and integrity.

Harmonious Meditative Thought of the Day

Today, I embark on a journey of forgiveness, extending understanding to my co-parent for lying to our children to protect their image. Forgiveness is an act of compassion and healing, recognizing that we all have moments of vulnerability.

Lies may have caused mistrust and confusion, but forgiveness empowers me to release the grip of anger and resentment. It's an act of self-compassion, acknowledging that we are all imperfect.

Through forgiveness, I create space for open communication and emotional growth. It's an opportunity to discuss the impact of those lies on our children and work together to rebuild trust.

As I forgive, I choose to be a source of honesty and understanding for our children, promoting harmony and emotional resilience. Today, I embrace forgiveness to foster a more harmonious co-parenting dynamic that values our children's emotional well-being above all else.

Deeper Connection Within

I forgive my mind for thinking I needed to _____
_____ .

I forgive myself for not being honest when _____
_____ .

I forgive myself for harshly judging myself for _____
_____ .

Loving Statements About Me

My heart is a canvas, and I am painting it with the colors of forgiveness.

I am cultivating a mindset of compassion and understanding.

I am releasing old wounds and embracing a new beginning.

Gratitude Reflection of the Day

Today, I am filled with gratitude for the unique journey of co-parenting, which has allowed me to embrace every moment and appreciate the love and growth it brings.

Inner Reflections

I Forgive You And Your Family For Attempting To Turn Our Children Against Me

Forgiveness Reflection of the Day

As I embark on a journey of self-reflection and healing, I find myself confronting the painful reality of a co-parent and their family attempting to turn our children against me. This emotional and psychological challenge has tested my resilience but has also become an opportunity for growth, self-discovery, and empowerment.

Admitting the existence of co-parental alienation is the first step toward healing. It's natural to feel hurt, angry, and betrayed by the attempts to manipulate our children's perceptions and emotions. However, I am proactively addressing and overcoming this problematic ordeal by acknowledging the situation.

Forgiving myself for any perceived inadequacies is crucial to this healing journey. It's easy to blame oneself for the situation or question one's parenting abilities. However, I understand that I am doing my best in a challenging circumstance, and self-forgiveness allows me to release the weight of guilt and focus on positive change.

To fully embrace healing, I commit to providing our children with a consistent, loving, and secure environment. While I cannot control the co-parent's actions, I can control my behaviors and responses. By remaining a steadfast and emotionally available parent, I create a foundation of trust and stability that can counteract the effects of manipulation.

Moving forward, I am determined to foster open communication with our children. Encouraging an atmosphere where they feel safe expressing their thoughts and feelings without fear of judgment allows them to process their emotions and form their opinions. Through honest dialogue, I can address any concerns or misunderstandings they may have.

Forgiveness also means letting go of the desire to retaliate or engage in harmful behaviors. While it may be tempting to respond in kind, I recognize that perpetuating negativity only adds to the turmoil. Instead, I focus on cultivating a positive and supportive co-parenting environment that ultimately benefits our children's emotional well-being.

In this healing journey, I am reminded of the importance of seeking professional support. Consulting therapists, counselors, or support groups can provide valuable insights, coping strategies, and a safe space to process the emotional challenges associated with co-parental alienation.

Moreover, self-care becomes paramount in the healing process. Engaging in activities that bring joy, practicing mindfulness, and prioritizing one's emotional well-being are sources of strength and resilience. Caring for myself demonstrates to our children the importance of self-compassion and self-care in navigating difficult situations.

Healing from a co-parent and their family attempting to turn our children against me is a journey of self-discovery, empowerment, and growth. I release guilt and pain through forgiveness, opening the door to positive change. By extending forgiveness to myself and prioritizing a loving and stable environment for our children, I am fostering resilience, trust, and emotional well-being. In doing so, I contribute to a co-parenting relationship rooted in respect, understanding, and nurturing our children's emotional health.

Harmonious Meditative Thought of the Day

Today, I embark on a profound journey of forgiveness, extending compassion to my co-parent and their family for attempting to turn our children against me. Forgiveness is an act of deep strength and healing.

Attempts to alienate may have caused deep emotional wounds, but forgiveness empowers me to release the grip of anger and resentment. It's an act of self-compassion, acknowledging that healing is a path of resilience.

Through forgiveness, I create space for open dialogue and understanding. It's an opportunity to discuss the importance of unity and the well-being of our children.

As I forgive, I provide stability and love for our children, promoting harmony and emotional well-being. Today, I embrace forgiveness to foster a more harmonious co-parenting dynamic that values our children's emotional health above all else.

Deeper Connection Within

I forgive my mind for believing _____
always _____
_____
_____.

I forgive myself for not _____
_____ when _____
_____
_____.

I forgive myself for judging _____
for being _____.

Loving Statements About Me

I am choosing forgiveness as a path to emotional freedom.

My inner strength guides me toward healing and forgiveness.

I am moving forward with grace and compassion in my heart.

Gratitude Reflection of the Day

I appreciate the opportunities for open communication and cooperation in co-parenting, recognizing that they are vital for the well-being and happiness of our children.

Inner Reflections

I Forgive You For Teaching Our Children Not To Express Their Emotions

Forgiveness Reflection of the Day

As I embark on a journey of self-reflection and healing, I confront the challenge of forgiving a co-parent for their actions that involve teaching our son to suppress his emotions and minimize his feelings. This painful reality has ignited a profound need to understand, heal, and empower our son to embrace his feelings and navigate them healthily and authentically.

Acknowledging the impact of a co-parent's teachings on our son's emotions is a vital step toward healing. It's natural to feel frustration and concern when confronted with actions that potentially hinder our son's emotional well-being. However, I am opening the door to empathy and growth by acknowledging the situation.

Forgiving the co-parent involves recognizing their experiences and conditioning that may have influenced their actions. While their teachings may be misguided, understanding that their intentions may have arisen from societal pressures, outdated beliefs, or their upbringing fosters a sense of empathy, even while addressing the harm caused.

Self-forgiveness is equally vital in this journey. It's easy to blame oneself for not intervening earlier or allowing such teachings to occur. However, self-forgiveness involves releasing the weight of guilt and recognizing that I am taking proactive steps to address the situation and provide our son with a healthier perspective on emotions.

To fully embrace healing, I am committed to creating a safe space for our son to express his feelings and emotions. By promoting open communication and active listening, I can help him understand his feelings are valid and essential. Encouraging him to share his thoughts without judgment empowers him to develop emotional intelligence and resilience.

Moving forward, I strive to model healthy emotional expression for our son. Demonstrating vulnerability and sharing my feelings allows him to witness that emotions are a natural and essential part of being human. By embracing my emotions and discussing them openly, I provide him with a positive example.

Forgiveness also involves addressing the co-parent's teachings through constructive communication. Expressing my concerns calmly and assertively allows us to discuss our son's emotional well-being. By sharing research and insights on allowing children to express their emotions, we can work together to create a more supportive environment for our son.

In this healing journey, I am reminded of the importance of patience and gradual change.

Healing is a process that takes time, and it requires consistent effort and understanding. By being patient with both myself and the co-parent, I can gradually guide our son toward a healthier relationship with his emotions.

Forgiving a co-parent for teaching our son to suppress his emotions and minimize his feelings is a journey of empathy, healing, and empowerment. Through forgiveness, I release the grip of resentment and create space for positive change. By extending forgiveness to the co-parent and myself, I am fostering an environment of understanding, emotional support, and growth. In doing so, I contribute to our son's emotional well-being and equip him with the tools to navigate his feelings healthily and authentically.

Harmonious Meditative Thought of the Day

Today, I embark on a transformative journey of forgiveness, extending understanding to my co-parent for teaching our children not to express their emotions. Forgiveness is an act of empathy and healing, recognizing the complexities of parenting.

Suppressing emotions may have caused confusion or emotional challenges for our children, but forgiveness empowers me to release the weight of judgment and resentment. It's an act of self-compassion, acknowledging the evolving nature of parenting.

Through forgiveness, I create space for open communication and cooperation. It's an opportunity to discuss the importance of emotional expression and well-being for our children.

As I forgive, I choose to be a source of support and emotional growth for our children, promoting harmony and a healthy, vibrant environment. Today, I embrace forgiveness to foster a more harmonious co-parenting dynamic that values our children's emotional well-being above all else.

Deeper Connection Within

I forgive my mind for thinking _____
never allowed _____which caused
me to _____
_____.

I forgive myself for not speaking up when _____
_____.

I forgive myself for judging _____
for being _____.

Loving Statements About Me

I am creating space for love and positivity by letting go of resentment.

I am choosing to heal, to grow, and to forgive.

My heart is a reservoir of love, and I am filling it with the waters of forgiveness.

Gratitude Reflection of the Day

I'm thankful for the resilience and strength that co-parenting has cultivated within me, leading me toward a deeper sense of self-love and gratitude for the experiences that shape my life.

Inner Reflections

Healing Forward

In the final pages of this transformative journey, we arrive at a destination where forgiveness and healing intertwine, shaping a co-parenting relationship that radiates with newfound understanding, compassion, and resilience. Completing the 21-Day Forgiveness and Healing Journal marks not an end but a beginning – a beginning of a rejuvenated co-parenting dynamic where wounds have been tended to, boundaries have been set, and the seeds of a harmonious future have been s.

As you reflect on the pages you've filled, remember that forgiveness is not a one-time act but a continuous process. Just as a garden requires ongoing care to flourish, so does your co-parenting relationship, which requires nurturing, patience, and dedication. The insights gained through this journal are the tools you can carry forward, shaping how you interact, communicate, and cooperate with your co-parent.

Forgiveness is not about condoning past actions; it's about releasing the emotional shackles that have held you back. It's about understanding that healing is an investment in your well-being and the well-being of your children. You've unlocked a door to greater emotional freedom through forgiveness, allowing you to embrace a more positive and empowered co-parenting journey.

Remember that healing is not linear. There will be moments of challenge and moments of triumph. But armed with the wisdom and self-awareness cultivated through this journal, you have the resilience to navigate the twists and turns ahead. You've acquired the tools to approach disagreements with grace, establish boundaries with respect, and prioritize the emotional health of yourself and your children.

As you move forward, continue to practice the art of forgiveness and healing. Keep your journal as a companion on your ongoing journey, using its pages to document moments of growth, reflections on challenges, and expressions of gratitude. Every entry is a testament to your commitment to creating a co-parenting relationship rooted in understanding, empathy, and cooperation.

Let us embrace the transformation that forgiveness and healing have ignited within us. Let us celebrate the progress and bridges built toward a harmonious co-parenting future. May this journey remind us that we can transcend pain and embrace growth. With open hearts and renewed spirits, let us move forward, guided by the principles of forgiveness, empathy, and self-care, knowing that our path can reshape our co-parenting narrative into one of hope, unity, and enduring love.

Thank you for embarking on this remarkable journey. May your co-parenting relationship blossom with each step toward forgiveness, healing, and a brighter tomorrow.

In gratitude,

Tuniscia O

Below Is A List Of All 35 Forgiveness Journals

Written By: Tuniscia O

Available on Amazon and other major bookstores or
www.forgivenesslifestyle.com
Instagram: @forgivenesslifestyle
For bulk orders: info@forgivenesslifestyle.com

Forgiving Yourself

Forgiving Your Body Journal

Accepting the Gift of
Forgiveness Journal

Forgiving People Who
Reject You Journal

P.S. Forgive Yourself
First Journal

Who Do You Struggle
To Forgive Journal

Forgiving Your Struggle
With Addiction Journal

Parenthood

Forgiving and Overcoming
Mom Guilt Journal

Forgiveness Journal for Fathers

Parents Forgiving
Tweens/Teen Journal

Parents Forgiving Adult
Children Journal

Forgiving Your Parents

Forgiving Your Mother Journal

Forgiving Your Father Journal

Forgiving Your Parents Journal

Family

Forgiving Dead Loved
One's Journal

Forgiving Family Secrets Journal

Forgiving The Bullies In
Your Family Journal

Forgiving Your Siblings Journal

Marriage

Forgiving Your Wife Journal
Forgiving Your Husband Journal
Forgiving Your Mother-
In-Law Journal

Romantic Relationships

Forgiving Your Ex Journal
Forgiving The "New"
Woman Journal

Teens & Millennials

Forgiveness Journals for Teens
Forgiveness Journal
for Millennials

Religion

Forgiving God Journal
Forgiving Church People Journal

Blended Family

Forgiving A Co-Parent Journal
Forgiveness Journal
for Stepmothers
Forgiving Your
Stepmother Journal
Forgiving Your Stepkids
Mom Journal

Relationships

Forgiving Your Abuser Journal
Forgiving Friends Journal

Business/Finances

Forgiveness In Business Journal
Forgiving People At
Work Journal
Forgiving Past Money
Mistakes Journal

Sending you loving energy as you
forgive, heal, and grow.
www.forgivenesslifestyle.com

Thank You

Gratitude is the thread that weaves connections, and at this moment, I extend my deepest appreciation to those whose unwavering support and love have been the foundation of this 35-journal writing journey and beyond.

To my beloved husband, your unwavering confidence and support during our marriage and this writing project have been my anchor. Thank you for your belief in me. It has been a constant source of inspiration. Your love and presence in my life make my soul smile.

To my mom, your honesty and vulnerability have led to this beautiful healing journey. Your transparency has supported my healing and given me the strength to support others on their transformational journey. I will forever be grateful for your courage to tell the truth.

My dear daughter, Shantia Dajah, your reminder to give myself grace has been a guiding light. Your wisdom transcends your years. You make my heart smile.

To my son, Damien, your encouragement and motivation have fueled my determination to embark on this transformative journey. Your presence in my life is a source of boundless joy.

To Ike, my youngest son, your cheering from the sidelines has been a source of motivation and warmth. Your enthusiasm lights up my days.

My sister, Tanniedra, your unwavering belief in me and our brainstorming sessions have been invaluable. You are truly a gift.

Little sister, Jazmin, your willingness to share your experiences and vulnerability has touched my heart deeply. Your courage is inspiring.

To my "business bestie," Martha Banks Hall, the Creator of Vision Words, your prayers, encouraging texts, and our deep explorations of thoughts have been a source of clarity and growth to help me birth this project.

Denise, my beautiful friend, "The Fertility Godmother," your enthusiastic voice memos have made me feel like a rock star. Your presence has been a pillar of my strength.

To Thuy, I'm deeply grateful for your accountability and sisterhood, and I hold you as the beautiful gift you are close to my heart.

To Georgette and Cristal, your cheers have lifted my spirits. Your presence in my life is a blessing.

You all hold a special place in my heart, and I thank you from the depths of my soul for being a part of my journey.

www.ingramcontent.com/pod-product-compliance
Lightning Source LLC
Chambersburg PA
CBHW071354120626
46546CB00002B/689